All Together

THE **FAMILY** DEVOTIONAL

All Together

THE **FAMILY** DEVOTIONAL

CWR

STEVE AND BEKAH LEGG

Concept development, editing, design and production by CWR.
Printed in the UK by Linney
ISBN: 978-1-78259-692-9

Contents

Introduction

I don't know about you, but I (Bekah) love an adventure. I love having adventures, reading about them in books and watching them on TV. I love the excitement – the moments when you're not sure what's going to happen, and the thrill when you see how a great plan is coming together to make everything OK.

Steve and I have had some pretty big adventures of our own. I've lived in Africa and visited remote islands; Steve has performed all over the world and climbed Africa's highest mountain; not to mention the five girls we've raised together! But the greatest adventure of our lives has been following Jesus.

It's easy to say it, but it's true. Getting to know God – the awesome, incredible, world-creating God – has been the most exciting thing we have ever done. There have been ups and downs, and moments when we had no idea what would happen next or how a situation could possibly be rescued. We've felt alone at times, scared at times and unsure of where to go. But God has always been there and He's shown us how to trust Him and follow Him.

For me, it all began when I was a little girl, aged just four, sitting with my mum and dad in the living room at home. I asked Jesus to become my friend. And He did. Ever since, I've been getting to know Him better, and it was my mum and dad who started me on that journey of discovery. Every night we would read the Bible together and pray, and I learned to love the Bible – and to even look forward to bedtime when I would discover something new about my friend Jesus.

The Bible is full of the most incredible stories and each one shows us something new about God. As we meet characters like Moses, Esther and David, we learn about them, but we also learn about God as we see how He loves them, how He watches over them and how He protects them. And all the way through, the stories are full of drama, suspense and rescue. Mini adventures within the greatest story of them all: the story of God and His great love for the world.

I am so grateful to my parents for teaching me to love the Bible and to know how to find God in its pages. Steve's story is different – he started following Jesus at a Boys' Brigade camp and his family weren't very happy about it. In a way, it's shown us how very blessed I was to have parents who introduced me to Jesus and encouraged me to know Him better. And that's something we both want to pass on to our own children.

Steve and I have written this book to help other families discover more about God together. Family time is under increasing pressure as work and even church commitments make us busier and busier. Children are getting more and more homework, and facing new and difficult situations at school and on the internet that make it easy for them to feel isolated and alone. But we were created to live and love together, to support each other and work out how to navigate the world as a family.

We hope that this book helps you to make God part of the family. Whether you choose to look at it at bedtime, at breakfast, on the sofa or over the dinner table, it's an opportunity to talk together and to include God in the conversation. Why not take it in turns to read each section or each day aloud to the rest of the family? The questions are there to get you talking – not just children, but parents too. Hopefully our questions will spark more questions and you'll get to know each other more as you learn about God.

Our prayer for you, over the next 12 weeks, is that you will grow closer together as a family, and that you will discover new things about each other as you deepen your relationship with God. We pray you know God's presence with you, not just as you do these devotions but in the details of every day, and that these 12 weeks will be the beginning of an incredible adventure for your family as you read about the greatest rescue the world has ever known.

Creator

Genesis 1:1–5,20–21

'In the beginning, when God created the universe, the earth was formless and desolate. The raging ocean that covered everything was engulfed in total darkness, and the Spirit of God was moving over the water. Then God commanded, "Let there be light"—and light appeared. God was pleased with what he saw. Then he separated the light from the darkness, and he named the light "Day" and the darkness "Night." Evening passed and morning came—that was the first day.

Then God commanded, "Let the water be filled with many kinds of living beings, and let the air be filled with birds." So God created the great sea monsters, all kinds of creatures that live in the water, and all kinds of birds. And God was pleased with what he saw.'

Something to think about

This is the very beginning of the Bible. In fact, it's the very beginning of the universe. God was there before any of it began. It's mind blowing. We can't even imagine what it was like. We can't begin to know how God did it. But we do know this – God is the creator of the universe. He made everything in it.

But more amazing still is that this same God wants to know you and me; the rest of the Bible tells the story of everything He has done to make that possible. It's the most incredible thing to know that this wonderful God loves us and we can be His friends.

Bekah says...

I love watching nature programmes with my children where we learn so much about God's amazing world.

Steve's interesting fact

There are about two trillion galaxies in the universe and there are about 100 billion stars in a galaxy. That means there are about 1,000,000,000,000,000,000,000 (that's one billion trillion) stars in the observable universe.

Something to talk about

· Where is the most beautiful place you have ever been?
· What does it tell you about God?

Bekah says...

Why not take a look at all the stars tonight? As you do, think about how amazing it is that in such a huge universe, God knows you.

Pray

Dear Father God, You are amazing. Your universe is beautiful, the best thing ever made. Thank You that even though we are so small in comparison, You know each of us and want to be our friend. Amen.

Just like God

Genesis 1:26–31

'Then God said, "And now we will make human beings; they will be like us and resemble us. They will have power over the fish, the birds, and all animals, domestic and wild, large and small." So God created human beings, making them to be like himself. He created them male and female, blessed them, and said, "Have many children, so that your descendants will live all over the earth and bring it under their control. I am putting you in charge of the fish, the birds, and all the wild animals. I have provided all kinds of grain and all kinds of fruit for you to eat; but for all the wild animals and for all the birds I have provided grass and leafy plants for food"—and it was done. God looked at everything he had made, and he was very pleased.'

Something to think about

The last thing God made, the icing on the cake, was human beings. People like you and me. But this part of creation was a little different to everything else. God had put stunning stars into space, He'd made incredible mountains and roaring seas, He had created delicate, beautiful fish, birds and animals – but He had something really special in mind for humans.

He made humans to be like Him. Not that we'd have the same nose, or colour hair, but that we would think like Him, love like Him and behave like Him. What's even better is that when He had finished making us, He was very pleased with the result.

Steve says...

I love building Lego. Every year I have a big project that I work on over Christmas with my nine-year-old nephew, Hudson. Last year we made the Millennium Falcon. It was an epic task and I was pleased with it when it was finished.

Something to talk about

· Have you ever made something that you were really pleased with?
· Can you describe how else you felt when you had finished? ·
· Do you treat or see it differently to other objects you own?

Bekah says...

I have heard too many children, and grown-ups for that matter, say that they wished that they looked like someone else – or they think that they're not good enough. It's important to remember that when God made you, He looked at you and was very pleased.

Pray

Father God, thank You for making each one of us. Help us to remember that You will always love us. Amen.

And... rest

Genesis 2:1–4

'And so the whole universe was completed. By the seventh day God finished what he had been doing and stopped working. He blessed the seventh day and set it apart as a special day, because by that day he had completed his creation and stopped working. And that is how the universe was created.'

Something to think about

God had been working really hard, making everything in the universe, but, when He was finished, He took a day out to stop, relax and enjoy what He had made. He also said that we should do the same (see Exodus 20:8–10).

People want us to work harder and harder for longer and longer – at school, at work and even sometimes at home. But God is not like our teacher or our boss, He wants us to work when it's time to work but know when it's time to rest.

Resting is really important. Everyone knows that we get grumpy if we get too tired, but true rest is about more than just that. It is also about enjoying what God has given us. It can mean spending time with each other, doing fun things and making sure everyone gets a rest – not just children!

Bekah says...

When I was a single mum, there was never any time to rest; my girls were small, one was ill for a very long time, so there was always something to do. But some friends at church were super kind and once a month would look after the girls to give me a break.

Something to talk about

· What do you like to do when you wind down?
· What do you like to do together as a family?

Bekah says...

Is there a family you know who could really do with a break - what could you do to help them?

Pray

Father God, thank You that You created us to rest sometimes so we can enjoy what You've given us. Help us not to forget to slow down and enjoy being with You. Amen.

Are you sure?

Genesis 3:1–6

'Now the snake was the most cunning animal that the LORD God had made. The snake asked the woman, "Did God really tell you not to eat fruit from any tree in the garden?"

"We may eat the fruit of any tree in the garden," the woman answered, "except the tree in the middle of it. God told us not to eat the fruit of that tree or even touch it; if we do, we will die."

The snake replied, "That's not true; you will not die. God said that because he knows that when you eat it, you will be like God and know what is good and what is bad."

The woman saw how beautiful the tree was and how good its fruit would be to eat, and she thought how wonderful it would be to become wise. So she took some of the fruit and ate it.'

Something to think about

Adam and Eve were God's close friends. They really knew Him. They walked with Him, they talked with Him; they could be with Him whenever they wanted. What a privilege. There was just one thing that God asked them not to do: He told them not to eat the fruit from the central tree in the Garden of Eden.

Even though they spent so much time with God, Adam and Eve easily forgot who He was and so were tempted to eat the fruit. The snake questioned whether God was really good, whether He was really true and whether He really wanted the best for Adam and Eve. They should have known better, as everything they knew about God told them that He is good.

Steve says...

Reading our Bible regularly helps us to remember how good God is. Throughout the whole story of the Bible, God's people kept forgetting how good He is and yet He never stopped loving them.

Something to talk about

- Have you ever had a time when you felt confused about who God really is?
- How did you remember that He is good?

Bekah says...

Why not write a list of all the things that you know are good about God to help you always remember?

Pray

Dear God, thank You that You are good. Please help us to always remember who You are, even when others try to persuade us to think differently about You. Amen.

Not my fault

Genesis 3:8–13

*'That evening they heard the L*ORD *God walking in the garden, and they hid from him among the trees. But the L*ORD *God called out to the man, "Where are you?"*

He answered, "I heard you in the garden; I was afraid and hid from you, because I was naked."

"Who told you that you were naked?" God asked. "Did you eat the fruit that I told you not to eat?"

The man answered, "The woman you put here with me gave me the fruit, and I ate it."

*The L*ORD *God asked the woman, "Why did you do this?" She replied, "The snake tricked me into eating it."'*

Something to think about

Eve ate the fruit, and then Adam did the same. It changed everything. They suddenly got embarrassed about having no clothes on and didn't want to see God. When God asked them what had happened, both of them tried to get out of trouble by blaming someone else. Eve said it was the snake's fault and Adam blamed Eve. What a pair of chickens!

When we've done something wrong it's always tempting to blame someone else to try to avoid getting into trouble. But that is not the answer. The snake did trick Eve but actually she didn't have to eat the fruit, she chose to. The same is true of Adam – and us. No matter who puts pressure on us, we must take responsibility for the choices we make.

Bekah says...

When my brother and I were little we would often fight. I would tell my mum that my brother had made me hit him because he was so annoying. That never made it OK! I had to learn to control my temper no matter how annoying he was.

Something to talk about

· When have you come up with an excuse for something you did wrong?
· When have you bravely admitted the truth?

Steve's interesting fact

This note from a parent has to be one of the best excuses for their child not doing homework: 'Please excuse my son for doing so poorly on the test. The hour he puts aside to do homework and studying every week was lost when the clocks "sprung forward" over the weekend.'

Pray

Dear God, help each of us to be honest about the things we do rather than blaming other people. Help us to learn from our mistakes. Amen.

Separated

Genesis 3:22–24

'Then the Lord God said, "Now these human beings... have knowledge of what is good and what is bad. They must not be allowed to take fruit from the tree that gives life, eat it, and live forever." So the Lord God sent them out of the Garden of Eden and made them cultivate the soil from which they had been formed. Then at the east side of the garden he put living creatures and a flaming sword which turned in all directions. This was to keep anyone from coming near the tree that gives life.'

Something to think about

This is one of the saddest moments in the story of the Bible. Adam and Eve have spoiled their friendship with God. Their bad choices meant they could no longer walk and talk with God every day. They had to leave the garden. It was the worst day ever. God didn't stop loving them, but He couldn't be with them in the same way anymore.

The amazing thing is, that from this point onwards in the Bible, even though humans keep making bad decisions, God started planning a rescue that will enable humans to know Him and walk with Him once again. Humans made the problem, but God came up with the solution. We'll find out more about that later.

Bekah says...

A year ago I was leading my first team to Kenya with the charity Compassion. I got to the airport, checked everyone in and then realised I had the wrong passport. I felt sick, but Steve jumped into the car and arrived just in time with the right one.

Something to talk about

· Have you ever fixed a problem that someone else made?
· How did they feel afterwards?

Something to do together

Problems are a normal part of life. You can think of them as huge problems that you just can't sort out yourself – or as an exciting challenge, like a puzzle to be solved. If you think you can't solve a problem yourself, you can always ask your family or friends for help too. Why not try to work something out together this weekend – like a jigsaw puzzle or a bunch of riddles?

Pray

Father God, thank You for loving us so much even though we sometimes make mistakes and ignore You. Thank You that Your love always finds a way to bring us closer to You. Amen.

WEEK 2:
AN UNLIKELY PRINCE
MONDAY

Danger

Exodus 2:1–10

*'a man from the tribe of Levi married a woman... and she
bore him a son. When she saw what a fine baby he was,
she hid him... she took a basket made of reeds and... put
the baby in it and then placed it in the tall grass at the edge
of the river...*

*The king's daughter came down to the river to bathe...
Suddenly she noticed the basket... The princess opened it
and saw a baby boy. He was crying, and she felt sorry for
him. "This is one of the Hebrew babies," she said.*

*Then [the baby's] sister asked her, "Shall I go and call a
Hebrew woman to nurse the baby for you?"*

*"Please do," she answered. So the girl went and brought
the baby's own mother... Later, when the child was old
enough, she took him to the king's daughter, who adopted
him as her own son. She said to herself, "I pulled him out of
the water, and so I name him Moses."'*

Something to think about

Moses was in danger even before he was born, simply by
being born at the wrong time, in the wrong place, into
a very dangerous situation. His family was part of God's
specially chosen people – the Israelites – and they were
living in slavery in Egypt. Their ruler was Pharaoh, and he
didn't want new Israelite baby boys!

God didn't think Moses was born at the wrong time or place. In fact, He had a big plan for Moses, which included a big rescue when he was a tiny baby.

This week, we're going to get to know Moses, learn about the mission God had for him and see how God helped him to fulfill it.

Bekah says...

Here's a crazy rescue story - when my granny was a baby, she had whooping cough and nearly died, but the doctor told her mum to hold her over a hot cowpat to help her breathe! It worked!

Something to talk about

· Have you ever been rescued from danger?
· If you felt in danger, who would you ask for help?

Steve's interesting fact

Is it a duck... or a dog? Did you know the Newfoundland dog has a water-resistant coat and webbed paws? It was specially bred to help haul nets for fishermen and rescue drowning people.

Pray

Dear God, thank You that You are with us all the time and that You are a God who rescues. Amen.

WEEK 2:
AN UNLIKELY PRINCE
TUESDAY

Angry

Exodus 2:11–14

'When Moses had grown up, he went out to visit his people, the Hebrews, and he saw how they were forced to do hard labor. He even saw an Egyptian kill a Hebrew, one of Moses' own people. Moses looked all around, and when he saw that no one was watching, he killed the Egyptian and hid his body in the sand. The next day he went back and saw two Hebrew men fighting. He said to the one who was in the wrong, "Why are you beating up a fellow Hebrew?"

The man answered, "Who made you our ruler and judge? Are you going to kill me just as you killed that Egyptian?" Then Moses was afraid and said to himself, "People have found out what I have done."'

Something to think about

Moses grew up in a palace like a prince, but really he was an Israelite. When he saw how badly Pharaoh treated the Israelites, it made him angry. Really angry.

We know from the Bible that God hates it when people hurt and abuse other people; it makes Him angry. So it wasn't wrong for Moses to be angry at the situation, but it was wrong for him to kill the man. Sometimes being angry about a situation is right, but it's important that we learn to deal with things calmly.

Bekah says...

This is a bit embarrassing to admit – but when I was little I was sometimes very mean to my brother. I would say really nasty things that I didn't even mean. One of the most important things I've learned is to keep my temper under control so that I don't hurt the people I love.

Steve says...

When you're feeling angry, counting to ten can help you to calm down and not say something that you would later wish you hadn't.

Something to talk about

· What things make you angry?
· How do you make things better again after you have hurt someone?

Bekah says...

Is there someone you need to say sorry to? Why not do that today?

Pray

Dear God, help us to do the right thing when we're angry. Help us to always be kind to those around us. Amen.

WEEK 2:
AN UNLIKELY PRINCE
WEDNESDAY

Learning to listen

Exodus 3:1–5

'One day while Moses was taking care of the sheep and goats of his father-in-law Jethro, the priest of Midian, he led the flock across the desert and came to Sinai, the holy mountain. There the angel of the Lᴏʀᴅ appeared to him as a flame coming from the middle of a bush. Moses saw that the bush was on fire but that it was not burning up. "This is strange," he thought. "Why isn't the bush burning up? I will go closer and see."

When the Lᴏʀᴅ saw that Moses was coming closer, he called to him from the middle of the bush and said, "Moses! Moses!"

He answered, "Yes, here I am."'

Something to think about

When we read this story, it makes us wish that God would talk to us that clearly. Although, if He actually did appear in a burning bush we would probably just be very scared!

We can all find it hard to hear God, but the truth is, God speaks to us all the time. We just need to get good at listening. God talks to us when we read the Bible, through our friends, when we're at church and He responds when we pray too.

Bekah says...

I mostly hear God speak to me when I read my Bible. As I read, sometimes I notice a verse in a way I haven't before and I know that God wants me to pay attention to what it says. I will read the same passage a few times in order to see what God wants me to notice.

Something to talk about

· Have you ever heard God speaking?
· What could you do to help you hear Him better?

Steve's interesting fact

Your ears never stop hearing, even when you are asleep. Your brain registers the noises it hears but often just ignores the incoming sounds, especially if you are in a deep sleep.

Bekah says...

It's important to remember to not just pray to God, but to take time to listen to Him too. Why not take some time to pray together and spend some of that time being quiet to see if anyone feels God is trying to say something?

Pray

Dear God, thank You for speaking to us. Please help us to get better and better at hearing You. Amen.

Waiting

Exodus 3:7–10

'Then the LORD said, "I have seen how cruelly my people are being treated in Egypt; I have heard them cry out to be rescued from their slave drivers. I know all about their sufferings, and so I have come down to rescue them from the Egyptians and to bring them out of Egypt to a spacious land, one which is rich and fertile... I have indeed heard the cry of my people... Now I am sending you to the king of Egypt so that you can lead my people out of his country."'

Something to think about

It's the beginning of another great God rescue. God had seen how Pharaoh was treating the Israelites and He wanted to rescue His people. This part of the story is years after Moses got angry and killed a man. At that time, Moses hadn't had the patience to wait for God's plan; instead he'd tried to change things by himself and got it really wrong. But God still made him a central part of His rescue plan for the Israelites. Isn't that amazing?

Sometimes it seems like God is taking too long to answer our prayers and it's hard to be patient. But the truth is that God loves us, listens to our prayers and always has a plan – even if we can't see it.

Steve says...

I find it really hard to wait when I have put fresh bread in the oven. It smells so good when it comes out that I don't like waiting for it to cool down - even though it burns my mouth if I eat it straightaway.

Something to talk about

· When do you find it hard to be patient?
· How could you practise being patient in those situations?

Steve says...

There's a Dutch proverb that says, 'A handful of patience is worth more than a bushel of brains.' What do you think?

Pray

Dear God, thank You for always knowing the best plan.
Help us to trust You and be patient when we have to wait.
Amen.

Good enough

Exodus 3:11–12; 4:10

'*But Moses said to God, "I am nobody. How can I go to the king and bring the Israelites out of Egypt?"*

God answered, "I will be with you, and when you bring the people out of Egypt, you will worship me on this mountain. That will be the proof that I have sent you."

But Moses said, "No, Lord, don't send me. I have never been a good speaker, and I haven't become one since you began to speak to me. I am a poor speaker, slow and hesitant."'

Something to think about

When God spoke to Moses and asked him to join Him on the rescue mission, all Moses could think of was why he wasn't good enough. But God knew that, with His help, Moses could do it. He had made Moses, so He knew what he was capable of doing.

It says in the Bible that God knows us inside out; He knows what we can do and He knows the things we struggle with. The Bible also says God has amazing missions He wants to do with us.

None of us are perfect, but God wants to do some amazing things with us anyway.

Bekah says...

It says in the Bible that God has given each of us different 'gifts' (see 1 Corinthians 12). Some of us are good at speaking, others at cooking, or writing or being friendly. We don't all have to have the same gifts. What are yours? If you find it hard to know what you are good at, why not ask the rest of the family to tell you?

Something to talk about

· Does anything make you feel you're not good enough to do what God wants you to?
· What do you think God would say about that?

Steve's interesting fact

Judit Polgár began playing chess in tournaments at the age of six. When she was 11, she defeated her first grandmaster. No other woman has beaten a men's chess world champion; she has beaten nine.

Bekah says...

Judit may have been born brilliant at chess, but she would also have practised hard. It's important for us to work on getting better at the gifts God has given us. What do you need to practise?

Pray

Dear God, it's amazing that You know everything about us and that You choose to use us in Your plans, even though You know we're not perfect. Thank You so much. Amen.

Saying 'Yes' to God

Exodus 7:6,13

'Moses and Aaron did what the Lord commanded...
The king, however, remained stubborn and, just as the LORD
had said, the king would not listen to Moses and Aaron.'

Something to think about

In this part of the story we have three main characters:
Moses, his brother Aaron and Pharaoh. Moses and Aaron
did just want God asked them to. Pharaoh said 'No'.

One of the great things about God is that He never
makes us do anything. He lets us choose. And that means
we can say 'Yes' like Aaron and Moses or we can say 'No'
like Pharaoh.

Pharaoh knew that saying 'Yes' to God would mean losing
all his slaves, and that would make life hard and so he
wouldn't let the Israelites go free. Sometimes God will ask
us to do hard things, but He will *always* help us if we say
'Yes' to Him.

Bekah says...

Even Jesus found it hard to do what God wanted Him to do. The night before He died on the cross, He asked God if there was another way to rescue the world (see Matthew 26:36-39). But there wasn't, so Jesus did what God had asked Him to.

Something to talk about

· When do you find it hard to follow God?
· What is the bravest thing you've done for God?

Steve's interesting fact

A carrier pigeon called Winkie was awarded the Dickin Medal for bravery in World War Two (yes, a pigeon!), for delivering a message under exceptionally difficult conditions and helping rescue an aircrew after their plane crashed into the sea 100 miles from home.

Something to do together

Why don't you watch the movie *The Prince of Egypt* (DreamWorks, 1998) together this weekend? It will help you understand the big story of Moses.

Pray

Dear God, as we get better at hearing Your voice, help us to be brave enough to say 'Yes' to You, even when it's hard to do so. Amen.

Protection

Exodus 12:1,7,12–13

*'The L*ORD* spoke to Moses and Aaron... "The people are to take some of the blood and put it on the doorposts and above the doors of the houses in which the animals are to be eaten.*

*On that night I will go through the land of Egypt, killing every first-born male, both human and animal, and punishing all the gods of Egypt. I am the L*ORD*. The blood on the doorposts will be a sign to mark the houses in which you live. When I see the blood, I will pass over you and will not harm you when I punish the Egyptians."'*

Something to think about

God sent all kinds of signs to show Pharaoh that he should listen to Him. He sent plagues of frogs, insects, hail and locusts – just to name a few. They did cause Pharaoh to sit up and pay attention, but he still wouldn't let God's people go.

So God sent one last terrible plague, which killed all the Egyptian's oldest sons. But God wanted to protect the people who loved Him and followed Him so He gave them a special sign – if they put the blood of sacrificed animals on their doors, it would indicate that theirs was a house full of people who loved Him and He wouldn't let any harm come to them.

Something to talk about

· Today we don't put blood on our doorposts to show we're God's people, but what do we do to show that we love Him?
· Can our friends tell that we follow God?

Steve's interesting fact

Found in humans and most animals, blood is super important as it takes oxygen and other nutrients to our body's cells. Blood makes up around 7% of the weight of a human body.

Bekah says...

What could you do today that would show people that you follow Jesus?

Pray

Dear God, thank You that You protect the people You love. Help us to be better at showing the people around us what it means to follow You. Amen.

Remembering

Exodus 12:24–28

'You and your children must obey these rules forever. When you enter the land that the LORD has promised to give you, you must perform this ritual. When your children ask you, "What does this ritual mean?" you will answer, "It is the sacrifice of Passover to honor the LORD, because he passed over the houses of the Israelites in Egypt. He killed the Egyptians, but spared us."'

Something to think about

God knows that we don't have very good memories; it's why He told Moses to make sure the Israelites didn't forget how God had protected them in Egypt. God said that the Israelites should have a special day every year when they remembered the way He rescued them from Egypt. He wanted them to remember how much He loved them and just how amazing He is at rescuing. The special day of remembrance was called Passover and, even today, Jewish people still celebrate it once a year.

Bekah says...

Long before I was born, my grandpa was very ill with tuberculosis. The doctors said they would have to take out part of his lungs, but his church got together to pray and, when the doctors went to operate, his lungs had been healed so they didn't need to! That story always helps me to remember that God can do amazing things.

Something to talk about

· Are there some special stories in your family that you can recollect to remind yourselves of how good God is?
· How can you make sure you don't forget the good things God has done?

Steve's interesting fact

We might think we don't remember much, but our brains have a gigantic 'storage capacity' for learning. Experts suggest that the brain can store 2.5 petabytes of data – that's a million gigabytes, or three million hours' worth of TV shows!

Bekah says...

Could you create a special way of celebrating something amazing that God has done for your family?

Pray

Dear God, You do amazing things – help us to remember them. Amen.

Facing the impossible

Exodus 14:5,13–14

'When the king of Egypt was told that the people had escaped, he and his officials changed their minds and said, "What have we done? We have let the Israelites escape, and we have lost them as our slaves!"

Moses [said to the Israelites], "Don't be afraid! Stand your ground, and you will see what the Lord will do to save you today; you will never see these Egyptians again. The Lord will fight for you, and all you have to do is keep still."'

Something to think about

It was a good job that Moses had already seen how good God was at rescuing because now the Israelites were really stuck. Pharaoh and his army were coming at them from one side, and the sea was on the other! But Moses knew that God was bigger than the problem they faced. He knew that God could still rescue them. Moses was confident that God had a plan.

Sometimes it feels as though we have got to an impossible place, but we need to remember that God is able to do impossible things – and He *always* has a plan.

Bekah says...

I love the words in Jeremiah 29:11 where God says, 'I alone know the plans I have for you, plans to bring you prosperity and not disaster, plans to bring about the future you hope for.' They help me to remember God is with me all the time. Why don't you write out this verse and stick it somewhere where it can remind you all that God has a good plan for your family?

Something to talk about

· Are you facing a hard or even impossible situation at the moment?
· Who can you ask to help you with it?

Steve says...

One of my favourite quotes ever is from the French author, André Gide: 'There are many things that seem impossible only so long as one does not attempt them.' Is there something you think is impossible that you could perhaps try to do again?

Pray

Thank You, God, that You are always with us. Help us to bring difficult situations to You, to see how You will work in them, rather than simply viewing them as impossible. Amen.

Thank you

Exodus 15:1,6–10

'Then Moses and the Israelites sang this song to the LORD:
  "I will sing to the LORD, because he has won a glorious
  victory; he has thrown the horses and their riders into
  the sea.
  Your right hand, LORD, is awesome in power;
  it breaks the enemy in pieces.
  In majestic triumph you overthrow your foes;
  your anger blazes out and burns them up like straw.
  You blew on the sea and the water piled up high;
  it stood up straight like a wall;
  the deepest part of the sea became solid.
  The enemy said, 'I will pursue them and catch them;
  I will divide their wealth and take all I want;
  I will draw my sword and take all they have.'
  But one breath from you, LORD, and the Egyptians
  were drowned;
  they sank like lead in the terrible water."'

Something to think about

It turns out that Moses was multi-talented. He wasn't just a
prince, a shepherd and a leader; he could write songs as well.
This is the song he wrote with his sister, Miriam, after they
had crossed the Red Sea with the Israelites. They knew that
they couldn't just keep walking; they needed to stop and

take some time to write and sing about how great God is.

How good are we at telling God He is great? Sometimes it's easy to ask Him for things but forget to say 'Thank You' and tell Him all the reasons that we love Him.

Bekah says...

When Megan, one of my girls, was little she threw her arms around me and said 'Mummy I love you and your glorious squishiness!' It was an unusual compliment, but it made me feel very loved.

Something to talk about

· What's the best bit of praise anyone has ever given you?
· What is the thing you love most about God?

Steve says...

Compliments encourage others. Through kind words, we remind people of their value and their talents. All of us want to be noticed - receiving compliments confirms that we are. It isn't hard to compliment someone. Saying simple things like, 'You're great at maths' or 'I love your Sunday roast' can make someone's day. Why not try it?

Pray

Take it in turns to tell God one thing that you love about Him.

Grumbling

Exodus 16:2–5

'There in the desert they all complained to Moses and
Aaron and said to them, "We wish that the Lord had killed
us in Egypt. There we could at least sit down and eat
meat and as much other food as we wanted. But you have
brought us out into this desert to starve us all to death."

The Lord said to Moses, "Now I am going to cause food
to rain down from the sky for all of you. The people must
go out every day and gather enough for that day. In this
way I can test them to find out if they will follow my
instructions. On the sixth day they are to bring in twice as
much as usual and prepare it."'

Something to think about

Those grumbly old Israelites forgot how good God is so
quickly! Even though God had kept them safe from the
plagues, even though He had saved them from Pharaoh and
helped them across the sea, they panicked because they
didn't have any food. Yes, it was a big problem, but God
had just performed miracles to rescue them – surely He
wouldn't let them die of starvation in the desert after all
that! This was a moment to practise trusting God.

Sometimes we can be a bit like the Israelites. When we
have a bad day, we forget that God is good all the time,

and we grumble about how hard life is. Sometimes life really *is* hard, but God is still good and we can trust Him to take care of us.

Bekah says...

Sometimes my children have grumbly days when they think everything is terrible. On those days, I ask them to tell me ten good things about their day so that we can thank God for them. They usually feel much happier by the end!

Something to talk about

· What things make you feel grumbly?
· What things cheer you up?

Bekah says...

Why don't you make a habit of thinking of five things to thank God for every day? Could you think of new things every day?

Pray

Dear God, thank You that even when we are having a bad day there are still things to be thankful for. Amen.

Rules for living

Exodus 20:3–5,7–10,12–17

'Worship no god but me.

Do not make for yourselves images of anything in heaven or on earth or in the water under the earth. Do not bow down to any idol or worship it, because I am the LORD your God and I tolerate no rivals...

Do not use my name for evil purposes, for I, the LORD your God, will punish anyone who misuses my name.

Observe the Sabbath and keep it holy. You have six days in which to do your work, but the seventh day is a day of rest dedicated to me...

Respect your father and your mother, so that you may live a long time in the land that I am giving you.

Do not commit murder.

Do not commit adultery.

Do not steal.

Do not accuse anyone falsely.

Do not desire another man's house; do not desire his wife, his slaves, his cattle, his donkeys, or anything else that he owns.'

Something to think about

Now that God has saved His people, He gives them some rules to live by to show that they are His. He starts by reminding them of what He has done for them – how He has rescued them – so that they know they can trust His rules (see verse 2).

God's first rule is to only follow Him. Sometimes that can be very hard; we can make other things more important than God – like when we'd rather play games or watch TV than spend time with Him. But we still need to remember to put God first in our lives.

Something to talk about

· What are the most important things in your life?
· How can you make God your number one?

Steve's interesting fact

There are some strange laws out there. Did you know it's illegal to feed pigeons on the streets of San Francisco, as the birds are blamed for spreading disease and damaging property?

Something to do together

The Ten Commandments were the rules for God's family. Take some time this weekend to put together some rules for your family. Think about how the rules can reflect the values you have as a family.

Pray

Dear God, we are sorry for the times when we put other things and other people before You. Thank You for still loving us. We choose to put You first today. Amen.

God's name

Exodus 20:7

*'Do not use my name for evil purposes, for I, the L*ORD* your God, will punish anyone who misuses my name.'*

Something to think about

This week we are going to take a closer look at some of the Ten Commandments.

Sometimes we hear bad language being spoken around us. Other children at school, other grown-ups at work – even our friends sometimes may use such language. Because we learn so much by listening, it can be really easy to start speaking the same way – almost without realising. But God asks us not to use His name 'for evil purposes'. It's hard to understand quite what that means, but we think God wants us to know that whenever we say His name, it should be because we're talking to Him or talking about Him.

Sometimes people use God's name when they're angry or surprised but they're not talking to Him. That's quite rude really isn't it? We wouldn't like people to do that with our names! If we love God, it's good to remember that, if we call out His name, He is ready to hear from us. We shouldn't be using His name for any other purpose.

Bekah says...

It's good to choose our words carefully. When I was a little girl, I sometimes spoke super fast. But it made it really hard for people to understand me. I'd come home from school and tell my mum a story about my day and then have to stop and start all over again! It was very annoying but it made me think carefully about what I said, and how I said it.

Something to talk about

- Have you ever said something without thinking and then wished you hadn't?
- How can you try to make sure you only use God's name when you're talking to Him or about Him?

Steve's interesting fact

God is not the only one with a name – we all have names. Jack is the most common name in nursery rhymes while Jaws is the most common name for a goldfish. Barbie's full name is Barbara Millicent Roberts.

Pray

Dear God, Your name is the best name in the world. Help us to always remember that, no matter who we are with or where we are. Help us to choose our words carefully and to use Your name in a way that brings You honour. Amen.

WEEK 4:
GOD'S TOP TEN
TUESDAY

Time out

Exodus 20:8–11

'Observe the Sabbath and keep it holy. You have six days in which to do your work, but the seventh day is a day of rest dedicated to me. On that day no one is to work—neither you, your children, your slaves, your animals, nor the foreigners who live in your country. In six days I, the LORD, made the earth, the sky, the seas, and everything in them, but on the seventh day I rested. That is why I, the LORD, blessed the Sabbath and made it holy.'

Something to think about

Do you remember that right back at the beginning of the Bible, it says that God made the world in six days and then rested for the seventh? He wants us all to follow the same pattern in our lives, as He created us with the need to take time out. None of us can just keep going. Eventually we run out of energy and need to recharge.

Without a good recharge, we stop being really good at what we do, we get grumpy and we find it harder to cope with difficult situations. No matter how busy we are, it's important we take time out.

Bekah says...

I like knowing that God doesn't just want us to work harder and harder; that actually it really matters to Him that we take time out and rest too.

Something to talk about

· What's the latest you've ever stayed up at night?
· How did you feel the next day?

Steve's interesting fact

In 1792, the French Republic made a new calendar that made a week ten days long. Each month had three weeks and then there were some spare 'complementary' days at the end of each year. It didn't really catch on.

Bekah says...

Why not plan a family day that takes you out of your normal routines, and that you can all enjoy? How can you make sure everyone in the family will get a chance to rest and relax?

Pray

Father God, thank You for loving us and wanting us to rest. Help us to be a family that looks out for each other so that everyone gets a chance to take time out. Amen.

Showing respect

Exodus 20:12

'Respect your father and your mother, so that you may live a long time in the land that I am giving you.'

Something to think about

When you respect someone, you admire them and you listen to what they say. We might love our parents, but we don't always want to listen to what they say – especially if they disagree with us! When we treat someone with respect, we talk to them politely, we are helpful and we are friendly. Even if we sometimes disagree with them.

God doesn't ask us to like everything our parents say or do, but He does ask us to respect them. That means that we should talk nicely to them, even if they ask us to tidy our rooms or do the drying up. It means we should try and do kind things for them and be helpful even when we'd rather be watching TV.

Steve says...

God doesn't only have something to say to children about how to behave with their parents. There are other passages where He talks to parents about how to love their children too (see Ephesians 6:4)!

Bekah says...

I used to fall out with my mum sometimes – especially when I was a teenager. Now I'm grown up, my mum is one of my best friends, but I now have five teenage girls who sometimes get cross with me. It makes me wish I had been a bit kinder to my mum when I was younger!

Something to talk about

· When do you feel grumpy with your parents?
· How often are you kind and helpful?

Steve says...

'I love you.' There's nothing better than hearing those three magical words, especially when they happen out of the blue. It's an expression you never get tired of hearing. Why not take time to tell each member of the family three things you love about them?

Pray

Dear God, You are the best Father there has ever been. Help us as parents to be more like You and to love our children well. Help us as children to be kind and helpful to our parents and to love them well too. Amen.

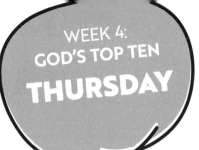

Hands off!

Exodus 20:15

'Do not steal.'

Something to think about

Today's verse is very short. But it's very important. God quite simply doesn't want us to take things that aren't ours. It seems that right from when we were babies, we had this tendency to take things that belong to other people. Even if it was just a rattle or a biscuit another person was eating...

God is amazing at not taking things from others. Even though He made us, even though He is the King and Creator of the universe, He doesn't ever make us give Him anything we don't choose to give Him – like our love, time or money. We need to treat people the same way and never take anything that isn't ours.

Bekah says...

Jesus met a man called Zacchaeus who had been taking other people's money for years. Zacchaeus realised he had been very wrong and chose to give people back even more than he had taken to make up for it. That's pretty impressive. If you want to read his story, it can be found in Luke 19:1-10.

Something to talk about

- Have you ever taken anything that wasn't yours?
- How did you feel afterwards, and did you do something to make it better?

Steve's interesting fact

When bees collect nectar from plants, they also help pollination (more flowers will grow) but some bees don't play by the rules. Bees that have been born with short tongues and therefore can't reach the sweet nectar have learned to carve holes into the side of a flower in order to reach their reward. This phenomenon, first observed by Charles Darwin, gets a bee nectar without the bee pollinating the plant. Cheeky!

Bekah says...

Some people end up stealing because their life is very difficult and they have no money. Is there something you could do to help a family who is struggling to eat? What about taking some food to your local food bank?

Pray

Dear God, thank You that You have never taken anything from us and that we know we can always be safe with You. Please help us to treat other people the same way so that they are safe with us. Amen.

Truth tellers

Exodus 20:16

'Do not accuse anyone falsely.'

Something to think about

This is another short verse – but it's very important. It basically means don't lie, don't make things up. We can make up stories for all kinds of reasons – to get us out of trouble or to impress people. Sometimes we lie to get other people into trouble, which is what this verse is concentrating on. It doesn't really matter what the reason is, lying is never a good thing.

Sometimes people talk about 'white lies', as if little lies are OK. Sometimes we exaggerate our stories to make them more exciting, but even this isn't good. The people around us, those we love, need to be able to trust us, to know that what we say is true and that they can rely on us.

In John 14:6 Jesus said, 'I am… the truth'. He wants us to be known as truth tellers too.

Bekah says...

In our house, we have a rule that children who tell the truth and admit when they have done something wrong get into less trouble than children who try and hide things. It's really helped them learn to be truthful. Is this something you do in your house?

Something to talk about

· When do you find it hard to tell the truth?
· What would help you be more honest?

Steve's interesting fact

As well as being the right thing to do, telling the truth is actually good for you. It's a proven scientific fact that people who tell the truth are healthier. They have less worry and less stress. They sleep better and feel better – and their relationships flourish. Being a truth teller is definitely worth it!

Bekah says...

Is there someone you need to tell the truth to? Perhaps you could talk to them today?

Pray

Dear Lord Jesus, sometimes it is hard to tell the truth. Sometimes we'd rather people didn't know when we've done something wrong, and may blame someone else in order to cover up our own mistakes. Thank You that You love us even when we make mistakes, but we are sorry for the times when we've not told the truth. Help us to be more like You and speak truthfully at all times. Amen.

Be content

Exodus 20:17

'Do not desire another man's house; do not desire his wife, his slaves, his cattle, his donkeys, or anything else that he owns.'

Something to think about

We live near the beach and we often walk our dog along the shore. Just behind the beach are the most beautiful houses, and we have thought about how much we would love to live in one. But it's unlikely we ever could.

There's nothing wrong with seeing beautiful things and admiring them, but it's very easy to start thinking that our lives aren't good enough when we do. Suddenly our house isn't big enough, our phone isn't new enough or we haven't got such good toys as our friends. But God wants us to learn to be content. If we spend our lives thinking about what we don't have, we will be miserable and it will distract us from living the adventure that God has for us.

Bekah says...

Magazines and TV shows are full of people who have been 'beautified' with makeup and stunning clothes. It is far too easy to compare ourselves to them and, if you're anything like me, you will feel like you come up short. But God made each of us and the only person we're meant to be like is Him. Let's not spend our lives wishing we were someone else.

Something to talk about

· Are there things that you think would make your life better if you had them?
· What do you have in your life already that makes it great?

Steve's interesting fact

I've often wondered what it would be like to be James Bond – travelling the world, seeing the most exotic places, wearing the nicest clothes and driving the nicest cars. Instead, I travel 45,000 miles a year, up and down the UK in my trusty Skoda. There are days I have definite Bond envy, but my car gets me where I need to go!

Something to do together

If you haven't already, plan the family day we mentioned earlier in the week. You could also make a 'gratitude box'. Write down things that you are grateful for in your lives and place these in a box (which you can decorate). You can then take out a piece of paper anytime and read out a reason to be thankful.

Pray

Dear God, help us to be content with what we have and to not spend our time wishing we were someone else. Thank You for all the good things You have given us. Amen.

What God sees

Judges 6:11–12

'Then the LORD's angel came to the village of Ophrah and sat under the oak tree that belonged to Joash, a man of the clan of Abiezer. His son Gideon was threshing some wheat secretly in a wine press, so that the Midianites would not see him. The LORD's angel appeared to him there and said, "The LORD is with you, brave and mighty man!"'

Something to think about

This story starts at a time when Israel had been taken over by another nation again – this time it was the Midianites. The Midianites were not nice – they went round bullying the Israelites and taking their things. We first read about Gideon hiding under a tree. He's trying to turn his wheat into flour without the Midianites seeing and stealing it. He's scared and feeling pretty pathetic.

Imagine how he felt when an angel suddenly appeared and called him 'brave and mighty'! He must have thought the angel had gone mad! He certainly didn't feel brave and mighty. But God had sent the angel with the message and God doesn't make mistakes. God sees things in us that we don't see ourselves. He made us, so He knows exactly who we are and what we can do.

Bekah says...

The first time I was asked to speak in front of a group of people, I was sure someone had made a mistake. I couldn't imagine being able to do something like that, but I asked God to help me and gave it a go and discovered that actually I could. Now I lead a church and speak all the time!

Something to talk about

· When have you discovered you can do something you never thought you could?
· How did that make you feel?

Steve says...

Gideon became one of the greatest judges of Israel. He was a strong opponent of the evil Baal cult. He defeated the Midianite enemies and appeased the Ephraimites. He brought peace to Israel for a generation.

Bekah says...

Is there a new challenge you can try to do today, that you've previously been frightened of trying?

Pray

Dear God, it's amazing that You made us and know us inside out. Sorry that sometimes we don't see ourselves the way that You do. Help us to know that with You on our side we can be brave and mighty like Gideon. Amen.

WEEK 5: FROM WIMP TO WARRIOR

TUESDAY

Where did God go?

Judges 6:13

'Gideon said to him, "If I may ask, sir, why has all this happened to us if the LORD is with us? What happened to all the wonderful things that our fathers told us the LORD used to do—how he brought them out of Egypt? The LORD has abandoned us and left us to the mercy of the Midianites."'

Something to think about

Gideon has a big question for the angel. He doesn't understand why God has let Israel be taken over by the Midianite bullies. He has heard the stories about how God rescued the Israelites from Pharaoh and he thinks God has forgotten His people.

It's easy to feel like God has forgotten us when things are tough. The truth is, sometimes sad and bad things happen, but it doesn't mean God has left us or lost us. Time and again in the Bible, God tells His people (and that includes us), 'Do not be afraid—I am with you' (see Isaiah 41:10 for example).

God doesn't ever promise that our lives will be easy or that He will make everything go just the way we want it. But He does promise to never leave us, to be with us when we're sad and to lead us into tomorrow.

Bekah says...

When I was 18, my mum got really sick and I was very frightened because I didn't know if she was going to be OK. I wrote this promise from God on a piece of paper and stuck it by my bed to help me: 'When you pass through deep waters, I will be with you; your troubles will not overwhelm you' (Isaiah 43:2). It reminded me that no matter what happened, God would help me get through it.

Something to talk about

- Have there been times in your life when it has felt like God has left you?
- How did you find Him in the hard times?

Steve says...

Why not choose one of God's promises to write out as a family verse and put it where you can all see it?

Pray

Father God, we are sorry that sometimes we feel as though we can't find You. Thank You that You are there even when we can't see You. Help us to know You more, and to trust You to see us through the toughest days. Amen.

Family traits

Judges 6:14–16

'Then the LORD ordered him, "Go with all your great strength and rescue Israel from the Midianites. I myself am sending you."

Gideon replied, "But Lord, how can I rescue Israel? My clan is the weakest in the tribe of Manasseh, and I am the least important member of my family."

The LORD answered, "You can do it because I will help you. You will crush the Midianites as easily as if they were only one man."'

Something to think about

God has a huge plan for Gideon; He wants him to rescue Israel from the Midianite bullies. Gideon is not convinced. Even though God has told him he is brave and mighty, Gideon can only see how weak and scared he is – just like Moses had been. But God knows that Gideon's strength doesn't come from the family he was born into, it comes from the God he follows. God promises to give Gideon the strength he needs, and that He'll make the rescue seem easy.

We get lots of characteristics from our families: things like the colour of our eyes, the shape of our nose and the curliness of our hair. Our families shape who we become, but they are not all that shapes us. Our surname might tell us which earthly family we belong to, but the Bible tells us that if we follow Jesus, we belong to God's family, too and that means that we can reflect His strength, His courage, His kindness, His love – and everything else that is wonderful about God.

Bekah says...

My brother, sister and I are like peas in a pod. I once met a man who knew who I was immediately - not because he'd ever met me or even seen my picture before, but because I look and talk like my brother!

Something to talk about

· What family characteristics do you have?
· In what ways are you different?

Steve's interesting fact

In 2016 there were 18.9 million families in the UK. That's a lot of families!

Bekah says...

Is there a trait from Jesus' family that you can work on today?

Pray

Dear God, thank You that You created us to be like You. Help us to grow the characteristics and habits You have, so that when people see us they can see the family resemblance. Amen.

Stepping out

Judges 6:25–27

'That night the LORD told Gideon, "Take your father's bull and another bull seven years old, tear down your father's altar to Baal, and cut down the symbol of the goddess Asherah, which is beside it. Build a well-constructed altar to the LORD your God on top of this mound. Then take the second bull and burn it whole as an offering, using for firewood the symbol of Asherah you have cut down." So Gideon took ten of his servants and did what the LORD had told him. He was too afraid of his family and the people in town to do it by day, so he did it at night.'

Something to think about

God's first task for Gideon was a tough one. Gideon's family had been worshipping other gods – the idols Asherah and Baal. God wanted Gideon to get rid of the family idols and burn them. This was nothing compared to what God had in store for Gideon next, but even this frightened him so he did it at night when everyone was asleep.

But that was OK. What mattered was that Gideon did what God asked. He trusted God enough to follow Him even though it was scary. Trusting God doesn't always mean that we're not frightened, and faith doesn't mean that we walk around carefree all the time. It means that we do what

God asks, even when our heart is beating so loud we can hear it. By doing this first thing for God, Gideon learned to overcome his fear and trust God more.

Steve says...

Eleven years ago, God asked me to create a Christmas movie to send to schools. I had no idea how I would pay for it or even how to do it. Around £250,000 was a lot of money to find, but I started the job. Over the next couple of years, God kept providing what I needed and It's a Boy! was finished, even though there were some scary days along the way.

Something to talk about

· Has following God ever meant doing something that you found scary?
· What happened?

Pray

Dear God, we each want to follow You. We trust You to know what is right and where we should go. Please give us the courage to do things even when we are frightened. Amen.

Too many

Judges 7:1–3

'One day Gideon and all his men got up early and camped beside Harod Spring. The Midianite camp was in the valley to the north of them by Moreh Hill.

The LORD said to Gideon, "The men you have are too many for me to give them victory over the Midianites. They might think that they had won by themselves, and so give me no credit. Announce to the people, 'Anyone who is afraid should go back home, and we will stay here at Mount Gilead.'" So twenty-two thousand went back, but ten thousand stayed.'

Something to think about

Gideon has become very brave and has collected a huge army of men from Israel ready to fight the Midianites. But God has a different plan. The Israelites had forgotten God and made fake gods out of wood and bronze. God wants to help them be free of the Midianites, but He wants them to remember who He is too. He knows that if a big Israelite army defeats the Midianites, they'll think they did it themselves, so God tells Gideon to let most of the army go home.

God loves to help His people, but He also wants us to realise that He has done it. He doesn't want anyone to miss out on seeing what a great and mighty God He is. Trusting God is scary sometimes, but it's so exciting when we see Him helping us to do things we never imagined we would do.

Bekah says...

God just kept sending more men home from Gideon's army - Gideon only had 300 men in the end and he'd started with over 30,000 (see verses 4-8). But God gave just those few men the most incredible victory and the Midianites didn't bother Israel again for years. Everyone realised just how amazing Israel's God is.

Something to talk about

· What's the most amazing thing you have ever done?
· How did it feel after you had done it?

Steve's interesting fact

A girl called Alex Scott was born with cancer and sadly died at the age of eight. But between the age of four and eight she raised over $1 million for childhood cancer research by selling lemonade!

Pray

Father God, thank You that Your strength is made perfect in our weakness. Help us to give You our weaknesses so that You can show how amazing You are through the things You do in us. Amen.

WEEK 5:
FROM WIMP
TO WARRIOR
WEEKEND

Not about Gideon

Judges 8:22–23

'After that, the Israelites said to Gideon, "Be our ruler—you and your descendants after you. You have saved us from the Midianites."

Gideon answered, "I will not be your ruler, nor will my son. The Lord will be your ruler."'

Something to think about

After all that God had just done, the Israelites still didn't get it. Even though God had just done the most incredible miracle, defeating the Midianites with just 300 men, the Israelites couldn't see it. They got distracted by the man standing in front of them.

We live in a world where people love celebrities. We watch them on TV, we follow them on Facebook and Instagram. We may even do that with Christian leaders. We start following the person instead of God. We sing songs in church, but it ends up more like a concert with a band than people coming together to worship our amazing God.

Gideon didn't want people to think he was special so he pointed them back to God. Let's do the same and remember that God is Lord of all.

Bekah says...

There's nothing wrong with admiring people and recognising their talents. But remember that the most gifted one of all is God – and He is the one who made those people and gave them their talents.

Something to talk about

· Who do you admire and why?
· How do you keep God first in your life?

Steve's interesting fact

Celebrities are a funny bunch. Here are four 'fascinating' facts about some of the biggest names in showbiz: Daniel Craig is the first actor to play James Bond who was born after the film series began. One Direction member, Louis Tomlinson, hates baked beans. Mr Bean star, Rowan Atkinson, has a master's degree in Electrical Engineering. Zayn Malik didn't have a passport before he was on *X Factor*.

Something to do together

Why not take some time over this weekend to thank God for the way He has made each of you? You could even each draw a picture of another member of your family.

Pray

Dear God, it's so easy to get caught up in admiring and following people instead of You. In everything we do, we want to make sure that You get the glory, not us. Amen.

Chosen

Esther 2:16–18

'So in Xerxes' seventh year as king, in the tenth month, the month of Tebeth, Esther was brought to King Xerxes in the royal palace. The king liked her more than any of the other women, and more than any of the others she won his favour and affection. He placed the royal crown on her head and made her queen in place of Vashti. Then the king gave a great banquet in Esther's honour and invited all his officials and administrators. He proclaimed a holiday for the whole empire and distributed gifts worthy of a king.'

Something to think about

This week we're looking at one of Bekah's favourite characters in the Bible, Esther. She was an ordinary girl who lived with her Uncle Mordecai in a town in Persia. She was one of God's people, but was living in a foreign land where God wasn't worshipped.

King Xerxes of Persia needed a new queen so he ordered that girls from all over the empire be brought to him. Out of all the girls in all the land he chose Esther. What an incredible honour! But even more incredible was that God had chosen her too. She didn't know it yet, but she was going to be part of another of God's great rescues. And that was even more amazing than being chosen by the king.

Bekah says...

God didn't only choose Esther, though she was very special, He has chosen you and me too. God has a plan for you that only you can do. That's pretty amazing.

Something to talk about

· Have you ever been chosen to do something special?
· How did that make you feel?

Steve's interesting fact

Our bodies are certainly special. Did you know that one human hair can support 100 grams? That's about the weight of two Snickers bars, and, with hundreds of thousands of hairs on the human head, it makes the tale of Rapunzel much more believable!

Pray

Father God, thank You for choosing each one of us. Thank You that You know we can do amazing things for You. Help us to remember that we are special to You no matter what else is happening in our lives. Amen.

Making choices

Esther 2:21–23

'During the time that Mordecai held office in the palace, Bigthana and Teresh, two of the palace eunuchs who guarded the entrance to the king's rooms, became hostile to King Xerxes and plotted to assassinate him. Mordecai learned about it and told Queen Esther, who then told the king what Mordecai had found out. There was an investigation, and it was discovered that the report was true, so both men were hanged on the gallows. The king ordered an account of this to be written down in the official records of the empire.'

Something to think about

This is where the story of Esther starts to get a bit like a spy movie, full of action and drama. Mordecai worked in the palace and overheard two men plotting to kill the king. He told Esther so that she could warn the king. Mordecai saved the king's life.

But Mordecai had a choice. He didn't have to report what he heard; he could have joined the plot. We're not usually tempted to join a murder plot, but sometimes we're tempted to join in other things that aren't a great idea. It might be as simple as messing around when we should be working, joining in with gossip or not including someone who is left out. It's important to think about the things we do so that we can choose to do the right thing.

Steve says...

I have to be really careful with chocolate – I LOVE it. When I see chocolate I want to eat it, even if it's not mine. Once I ate Bekah's Mother's Day chocolates. That was a bad decision – I haven't done it since!

Something to talk about

· When have you had to make a hard choice about what to do?
· What was the result?

Steve's interesting fact

The human brain is over three times as big as the brain of other mammals that are of similar body size, and is the centre of the human nervous system, controlling all our thoughts, movements, memories and decisions.

Pray

Dear God, thank You for giving us a brain so that we can think about the choices we have. Help us to think carefully about the things we do, and to have courage like Mordecai to do the right thing in every situation. Amen.

Pride

Esther 3:2–6

'The king ordered all the officials in his service to show their respect for Haman by kneeling and bowing to him. They all did so, except for Mordecai, who refused to do it. The other officials in the royal service asked him why he was disobeying the king's command; day after day they urged him to give in, but he would not listen to them. "I am a Jew," he explained, "and I cannot bow to Haman." So they told Haman about this, wondering if he would tolerate Mordecai's conduct. Haman was furious when he realized that Mordecai was not going to kneel and bow to him, and when he learned that Mordecai was a Jew, he decided to do more than punish Mordecai alone. He made plans to kill every Jew in the whole Persian Empire.'

Something to think about

Haman could not have been more different to Mordecai. Where Mordecai thought about others and made good decisions, Haman thought about himself and made desperately bad and wild decisions.

The king had just made Haman prime minister and ordered everyone to bow down to him. Haman loved it. But Mordecai wouldn't bow. Not because he was being rude, but because he knew God said not to bow down and worship anyone but Himself.

Haman's pride was hurt and he got so angry that he decided to not just punish Mordecai but every other Jew in Persia. Talk about overreacting!

Bekah says...

Pride is a funny thing. It's good to be pleased when we do something well, but it's important not to get too carried away. It helps to be aware of both our strengths and weaknesses.

Something to talk about

· What things are you proud of in your life?
· What are your weaknesses?

Steve's interesting fact

Mother Teresa spent her entire life helping the poor, sick, needy and helpless. I visited her project in Kolkata, India and heard how she would choose her shoes from the donation box. She always chose first so she could pick the ugliest and most worn-out sandals for herself.

Pray

Father God, thank You that You love us just the way we are. Help us not to get big-headed, but to be honest about who we are and to allow You to keep making us more like You. Amen.

Crisis

Esther 4:1,13–14

'When Mordecai learned of all that had been done, he tore his clothes in anguish. Then he dressed in sackcloth, covered his head with ashes, and walked through the city, wailing loudly and bitterly...

When Mordecai received Esther's message, he sent her this warning: "Don't imagine that you are safer than any other Jew just because you are in the royal palace. If you keep quiet at a time like this, help will come from heaven to the Jews, and they will be saved, but you will die and your father's family will come to an end. Yet who knows—maybe it was for a time like this that you were made queen!"'

Something to think about

Haman has arranged for every Jew in Persia to be killed! Queen Esther has a choice. No one at the palace knows she is a Jew, so if she keeps quiet she might stay safe but all her friends and family will be killed. Or she can go to the king and ask for his help. But if she goes to the king's chamber without being asked, he could have her killed. What a terrible dilemma.

Mordecai reminds Esther of who she is and that God always has a plan. He wonders, 'Maybe it was for such a time as this that you were made queen...'

God puts us in places and gives us the skills ready for the right moment. Let's always look out for opportunities to help and serve God.

Something to talk about

· Have you ever been in just the right place at just the right time to make a difference?
· What skills do you have that God could use?

Steve says...

I was doing street performances in France when our translator had to leave. I was having a disaster without her, as my French is terrible, but then an English teacher walked along – just the right person in just the right place – and helped us out for the rest of the afternoon. She wasn't a Christian but loved translating for us, and we were able to reach thousands that afternoon with our message.

Pray

Dear God, thank You that You have given us skills we can use for You wherever we go. Help us to look out for opportunities and to spot when we are just the right people in just the right place. Amen.

A God who can help

Esther 4:15–17

'Esther sent Mordecai this reply: "Go and get all the Jews in Susa together; hold a fast and pray for me. Don't eat or drink anything for three days and nights. My servant women and I will be doing the same. After that, I will go to the king, even though it is against the law. If I must die for doing it, I will die."

Mordecai then left and did everything that Esther had told him to do.'

Something to think about

Esther decided to do the brave thing and not just save herself. She decided to go and see the king, but she knew it was dangerous. She knew she might die. She was very afraid; there was nothing she could do to make it safe. But she knew someone who could.

Esther knew that with God anything is possible and her one chance of success lay with Him. So, before she did anything, she asked for His help and got everyone she knew to do the same.

Life can be frightening sometimes: things like scary tests, big interviews, new challenges – things we're not sure we can do by ourselves. But we can always tell God about the things that scare us. He loves to help.

Bekah says...

It says in the Bible that God's strength is made perfect in our weaknesses (see 2 Corinthians 12:9). That means that when we can't do something, it's a chance to show just how great God is.

Something to talk about

· What's the scariest thing you have ever done?
· What helped you to do it?

Steve says...

I hate heights - they really frighten me. But I used to do great escapes to help tell people about Jesus. Sometimes I would dangle by my feet from a 40m high crane in a straitjacket in front of crowds of people. It terrified me, but, with God's help, I did it.

Steve's interesting fact

Vesna Vulović, a flight attendant on Yugoslav Airlines, survived a 33,330ft fall out of an aeroplane in 1972. She broke both her legs and was paralysed from the waist down. Her recovery took 17 months but it didn't put her off air travel!

Pray

Father God, thank You that we are never alone. Thank You that You listen to our prayers and love to help us. Help us to be brave and to do more things with Your help. Amen.

Rescue

Esther 5:1–3

'On the third day of her fast Esther put on her royal robes and went and stood in the inner courtyard of the palace, facing the throne room. The king was inside, seated on the royal throne, facing the entrance. When the king saw Queen Esther standing outside, she won his favour, and he held out to her the gold sceptre. She then came up and touched the tip of it. "What is it, Queen Esther?" the king asked. "Tell me what you want, and you shall have it—even if it is half my empire."'

Something to think about

After three days of praying, Esther puts on her best clothes and goes to see the king. You can imagine her trembling as she walked into the room, waiting to see what he would do. If he held out his golden sceptre it meant she would live. If he didn't, she'd be taken away and killed.

God protected Esther and went on to rescue all the Jews. The little girl who grew up with her uncle had become queen and saved her people. What an incredible life she had lived, and all because she trusted God enough to follow His ways no matter how frightening that was.

God has an incredible plan for you too. It probably doesn't involve being a queen, but it will involve you needing to have courage to do the right thing, even when that's hard.

Steve says...

I like this quote from author Mary Ann Radmacher: 'Courage doesn't always roar. Sometimes courage is the little voice at the end of the day that says I'll try again tomorrow.' Yes, courage isn't always loud and dramatic. It can be quiet and dependable. Courage can be when you simply keep going.

Bekah says...

Telling our friends about Jesus can sometimes take courage. Can you be brave and find the courage to tell someone about Him today?

Something to do together

Can you find something brave to do together this weekend? Maybe you could climb a big hill or jump in the deep end of a swimming pool, or maybe you could tell someone all about Jesus?

Pray

God, thank You that You use each one of us in Your plans. We pray that You will help us to keep following You and give us the courage to keep going in Your great mission. Amen.

Foretold

Isaiah 9:6–7

'A child is born to us!
 A son is given to us!
 And he will be our ruler.
 He will be called, "Wonderful Counselor,"
 "Mighty God," "Eternal Father,"
 "Prince of Peace."
 His royal power will continue to grow;
 his kingdom will always be at peace.
 He will rule as King David's successor,
 basing his power on right and justice,
 from now until the end of time.
 The Lord Almighty is determined to do all this.'

Something to think about

We've read about a lot of rescues – the Israelites kept getting themselves into trouble and God kept sending people to help rescue them: Moses, Esther, Gideon – and there are many more. But God also sent messages through His prophets, telling them that one day He was going to send a greater rescuer than they had ever seen.

This rescuer would be more than just a man, more than just a king. He would be born as a baby yet would be called 'Mighty God', 'Eternal Father' and 'Prince of Peace'. His rescue would create peace not just for a few years, but forever.

That baby would be Jesus. It was the most incredible

promise for God's people, and they had to wait a long time to see it happen. But God sent many messages like this, so that when Jesus came, people would know that finally here was the baby born to rescue the world.

Bekah says...

There are hundreds of these prophecies in the Bible each foretelling a different part of Jesus' story. I find it amazing that God gave so many hints before Jesus was born - but I am very grateful, it helps me to be very sure of who He is.

Something to talk about

· What do you find amazing about Jesus?
· How does that make you feel?

Steve's interesting fact

Moko, a friendly bottlenose dolphin, saved a sperm whale and her calf by leading them off a sandbar in New Zealand in 2008. Moko often returned to play with swimmers. Perhaps he wanted to be a hero again!

Pray

Father God, thank You for having such an amazing rescue plan ready for the world. Thank You for all the ways You've helped us to know that Jesus really is Your Son. Help us to always be confident that Jesus is the Saviour of the world. Amen.

Given

Luke 1:30–35

'The angel said to her, "Don't be afraid, Mary; God has been gracious to you. You will become pregnant and give birth to a son, and you will name him Jesus. He will be great and will be called the Son of the Most High God. The Lord God will make him a king, as his ancestor David was, and he will be the king of the descendants of Jacob forever; his kingdom will never end!"

Mary said to the angel, "I am a virgin. How, then, can this be?"

The angel answered, "The Holy Spirit will come on you, and God's power will rest upon you. For this reason the holy child will be called the Son of God."'

Something to think about

This is the beginning of the Christmas story – the fulfilment of the verses we looked at yesterday. But this isn't a story just for December, it's a story for always. The best story that ever happened.

Mary was just an ordinary girl, nothing special. She wasn't a queen or a princess, she wasn't famous – no one really knew who she was. But she was good enough to be given this most incredible gift – to be the mother of God. What an incredible honour.

Most of us are pretty normal, special to our parents but not famous or royal. However, we're good enough for

God. He knows us, loves us and wants to give us the most incredible gift. He wants to give us Jesus. Not as a child, but as a friend and brother, so we can know Him too.

Bekah says...

I can still remember the moments when I gave birth to my children. I couldn't really believe that these little squidgy bundles of noise were mine. It was overwhelming, the best gift I could have been given. But knowing Jesus, being His friend, is actually even more amazing. Wow.

Something to talk about

· What's the best gift you have ever received?
· Who gave it to you?

Steve says...

In our house, we send thank you letters to people who have given us gifts. Why not write a note to God thanking Him for giving you Jesus?

Pray

Heavenly Father, You are the most generous Father. Thank You for giving us Your Son. Help us to be generous to others so that they can see Your Son through us. Amen.

WEEK 7:
GOD WITH US
WEDNESDAY

Recognised

Luke 2:25–29

'At that time there was a man named Simeon living in Jerusalem. He was a good, God-fearing man and was waiting for Israel to be saved. The Holy Spirit was with him and had assured him that he would not die before he had seen the Lord's promised Messiah. Led by the Spirit, Simeon went into the Temple. When the parents brought the child Jesus into the Temple to do for him what the Law required, Simeon took the child in his arms and gave thanks to God:

"Now, Lord, you have kept your promise,
and you may let your servant go in peace."'

Something to think about

Simeon was a man who loved God and who had followed Him closely all his life. He was given an incredible privilege – to be able to see the Son of God before he died. He recognised Jesus immediately. It must have been amazing for Mary and Joseph, as at that point they were the only ones who knew who Jesus really was.

As Jesus grew up, there were lots of people who didn't recognise Him. People who had read all the prophecies, people who saw Him do amazing miracles, but still didn't get who He really was. It seems hard to understand how people missed it, but we live in a world where people still don't recognise who Jesus is. We can know everything about Him and still not understand that He is the Son of God and can change our lives.

Bekah says...

I first recognised Jesus when I was just four years old and I asked Him to be my friend. I've been getting to know Him better ever since.

Something to talk about

· When did you first recognise who Jesus is?
· How did that change your life?

Steve says...

I became a Christian through the Boys' Brigade. I loved playing football there and so I was hooked from the beginning, but it wasn't until I went on a summer camp that I realised I needed to ask Jesus to be my very best friend and become a Christian. It was the best decision I ever made.

Pray

Dear Jesus, thank You for coming to the world to show us who You are. We recognise You and want to be Your friends. Help us to get to know You better and better. Amen.

WEEK 7: GOD WITH US
THURSDAY

Empowered

Luke 3:21–23

'After all the people had been baptized, Jesus also was baptized. While he was praying, heaven was opened, and the Holy Spirit came down upon him in bodily form like a dove. And a voice came from heaven, "You are my own dear Son. I am pleased with you."

When Jesus began his work, he was about thirty years old.'

Something to think about

Jesus had grown up like a normal boy, but this is the moment when everything starts to change and people begin to see that He is not quite like everyone else. It is when the Holy Spirit gives Him the power to rescue the world – and the moment when God lets everyone know that Jesus is His Son.

God tells Jesus He is pleased with Him and lets everyone around hear. Jesus hadn't done anything particularly special yet – no miracles or great stories, but still God is really proud of Him. Sometimes we think of God as someone who is a bit frightening but, in this moment, we see that God is a really proud dad.

God loves to encourage not just Jesus but us too. We don't have to be the biggest or the best, He simply loves us.

Bekah says...

When I was at senior school, we had whole school assemblies once a term. People would be given special awards in front of everyone. I always wished I could earn one of those awards, but I never did. But that didn't change how God felt about me. He was proud anyway.

Something to talk about

· When has someone told you they were proud of you?
· How did that make you feel?

Steve says...

Baptism might seem strange to people who aren't Christians, but it was God's idea in the first place. Jesus sent out His first disciples and commanded them to invite people to follow Him. Anyone who accepted the invitation was to be baptised (see Matthew 28:19).

Bekah says...

Why not take a moment to say things you are proud of in each other?

Pray

Father God, Jesus is amazing! It's no wonder You were proud of Him at His baptism. Thank You that You love us like that too. Help us to be encouragers, to speak good things about people and help them feel loved. Amen.

Followed

Matthew 4:18–22

'As Jesus walked along the shore of Lake Galilee, he saw two brothers who were fishermen, Simon (called Peter) and his brother Andrew, catching fish in the lake with a net. Jesus said to them, "Come with me, and I will teach you to catch people." At once they left their nets and went with him.

He went on and saw two other brothers, James and John, the sons of Zebedee. They were in their boat with their father Zebedee, getting their nets ready. Jesus called them, and at once they left the boat and their father, and went with him.'

Something to think about

Now the great rescue has really begun. Jesus is beginning to travel around to tell people about God and His plan for the world. First though, He looks for some friends to travel with Him. He asks the most unexpected people. He doesn't go for important people with lots of power or education. He goes to some fishermen, ordinary working men, and asks them to follow Him.

It was the most incredible honour, but, at the time, they wouldn't have known who Jesus really was. It was like a stranger asking them to leave everything they knew – their family, their job and their boats. The Bible says they didn't think twice; they dropped everything and followed Him.

Jesus wants us to follow Him to. We need to make a decision like these guys did – do we want to stay with the things we know or are we ready to drop everything and follow Him?

Bekah says...

I think the biggest, wildest decision I ever made was to marry Steve! I had only been friends with him for a few months when he asked me to marry him, out of the blue. I was surprised but I've never regretted saying yes.

Something to talk about

· What is the biggest decision you have ever made?
· How did you feel making it?

Steve says...

Sometimes, it's best to run your ideas by others. Really smart people have a good group of people they go to for advice.

Pray

Dear Lord Jesus, we want to follow You. You are more important than anything else in our lives and we want to spend the rest of our lives walking with You, wherever You take us. Amen.

Loved

Luke 7:44–47

'[Jesus said] "Do you see this woman? I came into your home, and you gave me no water for my feet, but she has washed my feet with her tears and dried them with her hair. You did not welcome me with a kiss, but she has not stopped kissing my feet since I came. You provided no olive oil for my head, but she has covered my feet with perfume. I tell you, then, the great love she has shown proves that her many sins have been forgiven. But whoever has been forgiven little shows only a little love."'

Something to think about

Jesus has been invited to dinner – at a very important man's house – but a lady comes along and upsets things. She's a lady that people don't really approve of anyway, but then she comes and pours super expensive perfume all over Jesus' feet! Simon, the man whose house it is, is outraged.

Jesus is thrilled. Yes, what the woman did is weird, but Jesus knows that she did it because she loves Him and wants to show Him in the best way she knew how. Jesus just loves it when we tell Him we love Him – no matter how we do it. We can tell Him in our prayers, sing it in our songs or show Him through the things that we do. That's called worship.

Bekah says...

We all appreciate being loved in different ways. I like hugs and people saying nice things while Steve loves being given presents and people doing kind things for him.

Something to talk about

· When have you felt very loved?
· Who loves you?

Steve says...

In Middle Eastern culture, feet (particularly the soles) are seen as the dirtiest part of the body, yet the lady in our passage kissed Jesus' feet and cleaned them with her tears and hair. What a powerful statement.

Something to do together

We each have ways in which we like to be shown we are loved. Why not go online and search 'the Five Love Languages'? Perhaps you could do an online assessment to see what love language you all speak, then find ways to show each other you are loved, using what you learned?

Pray

Dear Lord Jesus, we love You. You are so amazing and so kind. We want to spend the rest of our lives finding ways to show You that we love You. Amen.

Be a Good Samaritan

Luke 10:30–34

'Jesus answered, "There was once a man who was going down from Jerusalem to Jericho when robbers attacked him, stripped him, and beat him up, leaving him half dead. It so happened that a priest was going down that road; but when he saw the man, he walked on by on the other side. In the same way a Levite also came there, went over and looked at the man, and then walked on by on the other side. But a Samaritan who was traveling that way came upon the man, and when he saw him, his heart was filled with pity. He went over to him, poured oil and wine on his wounds and bandaged them; then he put the man on his own animal and took him to an inn, where he took care of him."'

Something to think about

This week we're going to be looking at some of the stories that Jesus told when He walked on earth. He told this story because He had been asked who we should love and show kindness to.

It was a surprising story for the people who listened because, in those days, Samaritans and Jews were enemies. No one would have expected the Samaritan to stop to help a Jew. But he did. He didn't care about what made the other

94

person different to him; he saw someone who needed help, so he showed kindness.

Jesus wants us to be the same. It's easy to be kind to our friends but we need to do more than that. We need to show love and kindness to everyone, no matter how different to us they are.

Steve says...

I was talking about cakes to the lady at the till in the supermarket the other day; she told me her favourite cake was a cream slice. Even though I don't really know her, I went and bought one for her – it made her day.

Something to talk about

· Has anyone unexpected shown kindness to you?
· How did that make you feel?

Bekah says...

Can you think of someone at work or at school who you could do something kind for today?

Pray

Dear Lord Jesus, thank You that You have shown great kindness to us, and did so even before we knew You. Help us to love the way that You love and to be kind to everyone we meet. Amen.

Building our lives on the rock

Luke 6:46–49

'Why do you call me, "Lord, Lord," and yet don't do what I tell you? Anyone who comes to me and listens to my words and obeys them—I will show you what he is like. He is like a man who, in building his house, dug deep and laid the foundation on rock. The river flooded over and hit that house but could not shake it, because it was well built. But anyone who hears my words and does not obey them is like a man who built his house without laying a foundation; when the flood hit that house it fell at once—and what a terrible crash that was!'

Something to think about

In this story, Jesus was talking to the people who followed Him around but didn't really follow what He said. If you've ever built a sandcastle, you know that you can make them look amazing, but when the tide comes in, they crumble and fall. No one builds a real house on the sand, as it just wouldn't last.

Jesus is saying, through this story, that our lives are a bit like houses. We can make them all beautiful, but, if we don't build them on good foundations, they will fall apart. Jesus wants us to build our lives on Him. If we do that, then, when tough times come (like the tide coming in), we'll keep standing firm because God can't ever be washed away.

Bekah says...

When I was a little girl, my dad used to make the most amazing sandcastles – he took it so seriously that he even brought a full-sized shovel to the beach!

Something to talk about

· What things do you rely on to keep you strong?
· Do those things ever let you down?

Steve's interesting fact

The biggest sandcastle ever built was created in Miami, Florida. It took two weeks to build, with a massive JCB digger. It was nearly 14m high and was built from 1,800 tons of sand. That is a serious amount of sand!

Pray

Dear God, we want to get to know You better so we can build our lives on Your firm foundation. Thank You that You are like a rock that can never be washed away so we can always rely on You. Amen.

Noticed

Luke 15:4–6

'Suppose one of you has a hundred sheep and loses one of them—what do you do? You leave the other ninety-nine sheep in the pasture and go looking for the one that got lost until you find it. When you find it, you are so happy that you put it on your shoulders and carry it back home. Then you call your friends and neighbours together and say to them, "I am so happy I found my lost sheep. Let us celebrate!"'

Something to think about

We love this story. We love how much the shepherd loves each sheep. He has a hundred, so it would be easy not to even notice that one was missing. It would be hard to know which specific one wasn't there. But this shepherd knows all his sheep and when one gets lost he goes to find it, bring it home and then throws a party to celebrate.

This is a picture of how God feels about us. There are more than seven billion people in the world. It would be easy for God not to notice the people who have got lost – the ones who don't know Him yet. But God knows every single person in the world – our names, our faces, everything about us – and just like the shepherd, He wants to bring each of us 'home'. He celebrates whenever one of us chooses to follow Him.

Bekah says...

Jesus said that He doesn't just know our name, He knows each hair on our head (see Matthew 10:30; He's counted them all!) - that's absolutely mind-blowing!

Something to talk about

· Have you ever felt like no one notices you?
· How does it feel to know God knows and cares about every part of you?

Steve's interesting fact

There are over one billion sheep in the world – most of them live in China. Sheep have a field of vision of around 300 degrees, which allows them to see behind themselves without having to turn their head.

Bekah says...

Why not share with each other something that makes each of you unique?

Pray

Dear God, we can't really understand how You can know everyone on earth – it's too amazing to get our heads around. But we understand that You know us, better than anyone else does, and that You care about every little part of who we are. Thank You. Amen.

Treasured

Luke 15:8–9

'suppose a woman who has ten silver coins loses one of them—what does she do? She lights a lamp, sweeps her house, and looks carefully everywhere until she finds it. When she finds it, she calls her friends and neighbours together, and says to them, "I am so happy I found the coin I lost. Let us celebrate!"'

Something to think about

If we lose something important, we make sure we find it. This lady stopped everything until she had found her coin; she tidied her whole house.

Jesus more than one story about things being lost. It must have really mattered to Him, just like the coin really mattered to the woman. Yesterday's story showed us that God knows everyone and notices even one lost person. Today's story shows us just how much God treasures us.

Jesus wanted us to know that, just like the lady, He doesn't stop until He finds us. We're not something He doesn't care about; He really, really wants to find us and keep us safe. That should make us feel pretty special.

Bekah says...

I am terrible for losing things – it drives Steve mad. I always have to look for my car keys. I find them in the weirdest places. Once I found them in the fridge!

Something to talk about

· Who treasures you and how do you know they do?
· How does that make you feel?

Steve's interesting fact

One of the most valuable pieces of treasure in the world is the Oppenheimer Blue diamond. It sold for $57.5 million at Christies in Geneva in 2015. Now that is precious!

Bekah says...

Sometimes we forget to make sure the people we love know just how important they are to us. What can you do today to make someone feel treasured?

Pray

Dear God, we don't always feel like treasure, but it's amazing that You say we are so special. Help us to remember that You love us so much. Help us to show that same kind of love to other people. Amen.

Welcomed home

Luke 15:17–20

'At last he came to his senses and said, "All my father's hired workers have more than they can eat, and here I am about to starve! I will get up and go to my father and say, 'Father, I have sinned against God and against you. I am no longer fit to be called your son; treat me as one of your hired workers.'" So he got up and started back to his father.

He was still a long way from home when his father saw him; his heart was filled with pity, and he ran, threw his arms around his son, and kissed him.'

Something to think about

Jesus told one more story about something lost. This time the story was about a child who got lost. But this boy didn't get lost by accident, like the coin, and he didn't wander off, like the silly sheep. This boy was really rude to his dad, ran away and wasted all the money his dad had given him. He didn't really deserve to be found (see verses 15:11–16).

But the dad in this story really, really loved his son, even though he had been rude, reckless and wild. So when his son realised what a huge mistake he had made, he found his dad waiting, arms open wide, ready to welcome him home.

This is another story Jesus shared to help us understand just how much God loves us and wants us to be with Him, no matter what mistakes we've made.

Bekah says...

It's hard to admit we've made mistakes sometimes. But if we want to make things up with people, or with God, it's important we admit when we've got something wrong. God doesn't wait to tell us off; just like the dad in the story He waits to welcome us home.

Something to talk about

· When was the last time you made a mistake and didn't own up straightaway?
· How did that make you feel?

Steve's interesting fact

Remember Thomas Edison, the guy who invented the first practical electric light bulb? He messed up and failed thousands of times while working on developing the light bulb, but in the end he succeeded.

Pray

Father God, thank You for this story, which shows us just what a great Father You are. Thank You that there is nothing we can do to stop You loving us. Amen.

Good listeners

Luke 8:5–8

"'Once there was a man who went out to sow grain. As he scattered the seed in the field, some of it fell along the path, where it was stepped on, and the birds ate it up. Some of it fell on rocky ground, and when the plants sprouted, they dried up because the soil had no moisture. Some of the seed fell among thorn bushes, which grew up with the plants and choked them. And some seeds fell in good soil; the plants grew and bore grain, one hundred grains each."

And Jesus concluded, "Listen, then, if you have ears!"'

Something to think about

A lot of the people Jesus spoke to would grow their own food, so He told stories about farming. In this story, the farmer's seed falls on different types of soil; some seed grows and some doesn't.

Jesus explained that the seed was like His words and the soil was like the people (see Luke 8:11–15). Some people listened to Him and let His words grow in their heart as they followed what they said, but others heard the words and then ignored them, so the words came to nothing.

We can choose what kind of listeners we are. Do we want to let God's words grow in our hearts or let them disappear?

Bekah says...

I used to be a maths teacher. The best way to help children really understand the method behind a problem was to get them to practise themselves. It can be like that with God's words – we need to practise doing what they say in order to really let them come alive for us.

Something to talk about

· Do you think you are a good listener?
· What helps you to remember things?

Steve's interesting fact

Being able to find information quickly on the internet is useful but makes you less likely to remember it. As your brain knows it can just access it again easily, it doesn't bother to retain it.

Something to do together

Try playing Chinese whispers. One of you think up a phrase, whisper it to another and so on until the last person, who says it out loud. How close is it to the original?

Pray

Dear Jesus, we want to be like the soil where the seeds grew strong and tall. Help us to take Your words deep into our hearts. Amen.

Being good enough

Luke 18:10–14

"'Once there were two men who went up to the Temple to pray: one was a Pharisee, the other a tax collector. The Pharisee stood apart by himself and prayed, 'I thank you, God, that I am not greedy, dishonest, or an adulterer, like everybody else. I thank you that I am not like that tax collector over there. I fast two days a week, and I give you one tenth of all my income.' But the tax collector stood at a distance and would not even raise his face to heaven, but beat on his breast and said, 'God, have pity on me, a sinner!' I tell you," said Jesus, "the tax collector, and not the Pharisee, was in the right with God when he went home.""

Something to think about

This week we are continuing to look at some of the things Jesus said. There are two very different men in this story. The Pharisee was a really good man who did everything he could to follow God. The other, the tax collector, worked for the enemy and stole people's money. It seems obvious who God would think was the great one.

But Jesus had a habit of surprising people. The Pharisee comes to the Temple to tell God all the things he's done to make himself good enough, but the truth is, none of us can

make ourselves good enough. The tax collector knew that –
and he comes begging God to make him right.

The tax collector had it right, as the only way we can
be friends with God is if we let Him give us His gift of
'goodness'. We can never do it by ourselves.

Bekah says...

It's a relief to know we don't have to be perfect to know God. No matter how hard I try, I never manage to get through the day without messing up.

Something to talk about

· Are there things you do because you think it will make
  you right with God?
· How does the tax collector's prayer make you think
  differently?

Steve's interesting fact

Atelophobia is the fear of imperfection. People who
have it just need everything to be perfect!

Pray

Dear God, we're glad it's not up to us to be perfect. Thank You
that, through Jesus, You make us right with You. Amen.

Party invitation

Luke 14:16–20

'There was once a man who was giving a great feast to which he invited many people. When it was time for the feast, he sent his servant to tell his guests, "Come, everything is ready!" But they all began, one after another, to make excuses. The first one told the servant, "I have bought a field and must go and look at it; please accept my apologies." Another one said, "I have bought five pairs of oxen and am on my way to try them out; please accept my apologies." Another one said, "I have just gotten married, and for that reason I cannot come."'

Something to think about

Sometimes the Bible talks about heaven as being like a banquet – a big party. And it's a party we're all invited to. But we get to choose if we want to go.

In this story, all the man's friends have other things going on – things that seemed more important: a new field, new cows, a new wife – so they chose not to go. What happens next is that the man sends out more invites to other people, and they all come and enjoy the banquet while his friends miss out (see verses 21–24).

Jesus invites us to follow Him and be part of His great party.

Bekah says...

We can be easily distracted by other things – new friends, new toys, a new job, but let's not ignore Jesus' invitation and miss out on the party.

Something to talk about

· What kind of parties do you enjoy?
· What distracts you from replying to Jesus' invite?

Steve's interesting fact

The record for the longest dance party was in Ireland and began on 27 October 2006 at 12pm with 40 dancers. There were still 31 dancing after 55 hours. I bet they had tired legs afterwards!

Bekah says...

There is nothing like an invitation to make someone feel a bit special. It's lovely to be chosen to join in. Why not invite someone to spend time with you so that they know they are important to you?

Pray

Dear God, thank You for our invitation to Your party. Nothing could be more important than being with You, we'd love to come. Amen.

Judging

Matthew 7:1–5

'Do not judge others, so that God will not judge you, for God will judge you in the same way you judge others, and he will apply to you the same rules you apply to others. Why, then, do you look at the speck in your brother's eye and pay no attention to the log in your own eye? How dare you say to your brother, "Please, let me take that speck out of your eye," when you have a log in your own eye? You hypocrite! First take the log out of your own eye, and then you will be able to see clearly to take the speck out of your brother's eye.'

Something to think about

'Hypocrite' is a strong word. It's used to describe someone who pretends to be something they're not. One thing it means is moaning about somebody else doing something that you do yourself. In our family we call it 'the pot calling the kettle black'. Jesus told people with a log in their eye that they should not complain about people who have sawdust in theirs.

All that wood in the eye sounds quite painful, but really Jesus was saying that it's no good getting upset about your friend gossiping about you if you are a gossip too. Or it's no good being angry with your brother for being grumpy if you are being grumpy too. Jesus was quite strict about this – He said that if you go around judging other people, God will do the same to you.

Bekah says...

We shouldn't spend our time worrying about what other people are doing wrong. Instead we should concentrate on how we can be kinder, more generous and more loving.

Something to talk about

· What kind of things wind you up?
· Do you ever do those things yourself?

Steve's interesting fact

The word hypocrite actually comes from the Greek word *hypokrites*, which means 'an actor' or 'a stage player'. Actors in ancient Greek theatre wore large masks in order to play their parts.

Bekah says...

Is there someone who you struggle to see the good in? Why not ask the rest of the family to help you write a list of things that are good about them?

Pray

Father God, we don't want to spend our lives picking fault with other people. Help us see the good in them and help us be the kind of people we'd like to spend time with. Amen.

Forgiving

Matthew 18:23–27

'Once there was a king who decided to check on his servants' accounts. He had just begun to do so when one of them was brought in who owed him millions of dollars. The servant did not have enough to pay his debt, so the king ordered him to be sold as a slave, with his wife and his children and all that he had, in order to pay the debt. The servant fell on his knees before the king. "Be patient with me," he begged, "and I will pay you everything!" The king felt sorry for him, so he forgave him the debt and let him go.'

Something to think about

This is a story about a very kind king. His servant owes him more money than you can even imagine! But instead of throwing the servant in jail, the king lets him off. Amazing.

You would think the servant would be so grateful that he would treat others in a similar way. But, instead, the servant then goes out and demands money back from his friend and, when he can't pay, he has him thrown in jail. Unbelievable! When the king hears, he is furious and changes his mind about the servant. He can't believe the servant could be so unforgiving after he had been forgiven so much himself (see verses 28–35).

Jesus said that we have to be careful not to be like the servant. God has forgiven everything we have ever done wrong. Amazing. But that should make us treat other people the same way. We need to be able to forgive other people when they hurt us or make mistakes.

Steve says...

Forgiving can be very difficult, but it doesn't mean you need to say that what happened didn't matter or didn't hurt. Forgiving does mean choosing not to hold something against someone anymore.

Something to talk about

· Has there been a time when you have had to forgive something very difficult?
· What helped you to forgive?

Bekah says...

Is there someone or something that you need to forgive at the moment?

Pray

Father God, thank You that when we come to You with our mistakes, You always forgive us. Help us to be like You and to forgive people who do things that upset us. Amen.

Get ready

Luke 12:35–40

'Be ready for whatever comes, dressed for action and with your lamps lit, like servants who are waiting for their master to come back from a wedding feast. When he comes and knocks, they will open the door for him at once. How happy are those servants whose master finds them awake and ready when he returns! I tell you, he will take off his coat, have them sit down, and will wait on them. How happy they are if he finds them ready, even if he should come at midnight or even later! And you can be sure that if the owner of a house knew the time when the thief would come, he would not let the thief break into his house. And you, too, must be ready, because the Son of Man will come at an hour when you are not expecting him.'

Something to think about

When Jesus was born, and in the years afterwards, most people didn't know who He was. They either weren't expecting Him, or thought He would look different. They hadn't been paying attention to the messages about the Messiah who God would send to save the world.

It's hard to imagine missing the Son of God, but Jesus says that people will miss Him again. After He rose from the dead, Jesus went back to heaven but He promised that one day He would return to earth to gather all His followers to

Him. We want to be ready, as we definitely do *not* want to miss that! We want to be like the servants in this story who had done everything they could to be ready for when their master returned.

Bekah says...

The lovely thing about being ready for Jesus is that there's not much to do - we just need to follow Him day by day.

Something to talk about

· Have you ever been caught not ready for something important?
· How did that make you feel?

Steve says...

Are you ready for Jesus? Don't put off following Him.

Pray

Dear Lord Jesus, it's exciting that one day You will come back to take us to be with You forever. We want to be ready for when You come. We want to follow You and shine Your light while we wait for that day. Amen.

Showing kindness

Matthew 25:35–40

"'I was hungry and you fed me, thirsty and you gave me a drink; I was a stranger and you received me in your homes, naked and you clothed me; I was sick and you took care of me, in prison and you visited me." The righteous will then answer him, "When, Lord, did we ever see you hungry and feed you, or thirsty and give you a drink? When did we ever see you a stranger and welcome you in our homes, or naked and clothe you? When did we ever see you sick or in prison, and visit you?" The King will reply, "I tell you, whenever you did this for one of the least important of these followers of mine, you did it for me!"'

Something to think about

This is another story Jesus tells about the end of time when He comes back to gather His followers. He starts by saying that He will divide everyone into two groups – those who have looked after Him and those who haven't (see verses 31–33).

But it's not that simple. All of us would find it easy to do kind things if we saw Jesus face to face, but this story shows that actually it's not always like that. Jesus says it's about being kind to anyone and everyone. When we give food to someone who is hungry, we do it for Jesus.

When we give clothes to someone who doesn't have any, we do it for Jesus.

Bekah says...

When I was a single mum, some people from my local church came and helped me decorate my house and gave me furniture. Their kindness showed me they loved me, but it also showed me that God was taking care of me.

Something to talk about

- Have you ever done something kind for a stranger who was in need?
- Have you seen God taking care of you through His people?

Something to do together

Take some time this weekend to think together about how you can do something practical to feed the hungry, clothe the poor or welcome a stranger. Then go and do it!

Pray

Father God, thank You that we are never alone, that You work through Your people to provide for our needs. Help us to be You to other people, and to be good at taking Your love to those who need it most. Amen.

Let down

Matthew 26:47–50

'Jesus was still speaking when Judas, one of the twelve disciples, arrived. With him was a large crowd armed with swords and clubs and sent by the chief priests and the elders. The traitor had given the crowd a signal: "The man I kiss is the one you want. Arrest him!"

Judas went straight to Jesus and said, "Peace be with you, Teacher," and kissed him.

Jesus answered, "Be quick about it, friend!"

Then they came up, arrested Jesus, and held him tight.'

Something to think about

Jesus had spent three years travelling with His best friends the disciples. They had eaten together and visited people together. They'd seen incredible things and He'd told them everything about His Father and His plans. Yet one of His friends didn't get it. Judas had seen everything and yet, for some reason, chose to betray Jesus.

We don't really know why Judas did it, but he chose to hand Jesus over to the priests and leaders who hated Him. But here's the thing, Jesus still called Him friend. In fact, Jesus had known all along that Judas would betray Him and yet Jesus never sent him away, talked rudely to him or tried to stop him.

Jesus knows that there will be times when we let Him down but He loves us anyway and will always give us a chance to make up for it.

Bekah says...

Peter let Jesus down too, right after Judas. He told people three times that he didn't even know who Jesus was (see verses 69-75). Later he got a chance to tell Jesus three times that he loved Him, and then he spent the rest of his life telling people all about Jesus.

Something to talk about

· Has anyone ever let you down?
· Did you give them a chance to make it up?

Steve says...

None of the disciples suspected Judas. He was a trusted member of the Twelve. Even at the Last Supper, when Jesus told Judas, 'Hurry and do what you must!' (John 13:27), the others at the table simply thought Judas had been sent to buy more food or to give something to charity.

Pray

Dear Lord Jesus, You are the most incredible friend who loves us even when You know we'll let You down. Thank You for giving us a second chance. Help us to love You better. Amen.

Teased

Matthew 27:27–31

'Then Pilate's soldiers took Jesus into the governor's palace, and the whole company gathered around him. They stripped off his clothes and put a scarlet robe on him. Then they made a crown out of thorny branches and placed it on his head, and put a stick in his right hand; then they knelt before him and made fun of him. "Long live the King of the Jews!" they said. They spat on him, and took the stick and hit him over the head. When they had finished making fun of him, they took the robe off and put his own clothes back on him. Then they led him out to crucify him.'

Something to think about

This part of Jesus' story is very, very sad. Jesus is the Son of God, Creator of the universe, Prince of Peace, yet, at this point in the story, no one is recognising Him. Instead they are teasing Him and hurting Him and treating Him as if He is nothing.

It is amazing that God should send His Son to earth and allow people to treat Him like this. But it was all part of the rescue plan. It was the only thing that would work; if God stopped people hurting Jesus, He couldn't rescue us and He loves us so much that He decided it was worth it. How amazing is that?

Bekah says...

I got teased at school sometimes because I was a Christian. This part of Jesus' story helped me, because it showed me that Jesus knew exactly how I felt because He'd been teased too. I knew that if He could do that for me, I could cope with some teasing for Him.

Something to talk about

· Have you ever been teased?
· How did you cope?

Steve's interesting fact

The thorn plant, which was used to make the crown of thorns that was placed upon the head of Jesus, is believed to be a plant called *Euphorbia milii*. It was originally from Madagascar, but was then grown in the Middle East too. The plant is also known as Crown of Thorns.

Pray

Dear Lord Jesus, we know that You are Lord of all, so it makes us sad that these men didn't. Thank You for loving us so much that You would do anything to rescue us. Amen.

Killed... for us

Matthew 27:45–50

'At noon the whole country was covered with darkness, which lasted for three hours. At about three o'clock Jesus cried out with a loud shout, "Eli, Eli, lema sabachthani?" which means, "My God, my God, why did you abandon me?"

Some of the people standing there heard him and said, "He is calling for Elijah!" One of them ran up at once, took a sponge, soaked it in cheap wine, put it on the end of a stick, and tried to make him drink it.

But the others said, "Wait, let us see if Elijah is coming to save him!"

Jesus again gave a loud cry and breathed his last.'

Something to think about

This passage describes the saddest day in history; the day Jesus was killed. The earth even went dark in response. But it was one of the most important days in history too, because this was the day that the greatest rescue began for real. It's hard to understand, but Jesus died to save you and to save me. He died to save everyone who would choose to recognise and follow Him.

The things we do wrong separate us from God because He is perfect, but when Jesus died He took the punishment for everything we've ever done, and will do, and made a way for us to be close to God. He died and was separated from God so that we don't have to be. How amazing He is!

Bekah says...

When I was a single mum I didn't really have enough money. One day I had a big bill I just couldn't pay. A friend of mine decided to pay it for me and didn't want the money back. It was my bill but he paid it.

Something to talk about

· Has anyone ever done something amazing for you?
· How did that leave you feeling?

Steve says...

Jesus died for you. But He will never make you follow Him; He waits for you to decide for yourself. Have you made that decision?

Pray

Dear Lord Jesus, You are our very best friend. You did everything for us; You even died on a cross so our mistakes don't have to separate us from You. Thank You. We choose to recognise You as God and to follow You always. Amen.

The best news

Matthew 28:5–10

'The angel spoke to the women. "You must not be afraid,"
he said. "I know you are looking for Jesus, who was
crucified. He is not here; he has been raised, just as he
said. Come here and see the place where he was lying. Go
quickly now, and tell his disciples, 'He has been raised from
death, and now he is going to Galilee ahead of you; there
you will see him!' Remember what I have told you."

So they left the tomb in a hurry, afraid and yet filled with
joy, and ran to tell his disciples.

Suddenly Jesus met them and said, "Peace be with you."
They came up to him, took hold of his feet, and worshipped
him. "Do not be afraid," Jesus said to them. "Go and tell my
brothers to go to Galilee, and there they will see me."'

Something to think about

The rescue mission is complete. Jesus died to take away the
consequences of the bad things we do, but He didn't stay
dead. Jesus is the Son of God; He was there when the world
was made, He is the King of kings and the Lord of lords.
Nothing is more powerful than Him. Not even death.

When Jesus' friends went to see His grave they couldn't
find Him there. Imagine how confused those women
would have been to begin with, but then how excited they

would have been to see Jesus again. They started their day thinking everything was over, but then they discovered that Jesus was more than they had ever realised – He was alive again! The world would never be the same again...

Bekah says...

Some of the best news I have ever heard was after my mum went into hospital to have a big operation on her brain. When she came home safe and sound I wanted to tell everyone.

Something to talk about

· What is the best news you have ever wanted to share?
· How did you tell people?

Steve says...

Good news is always for sharing. We must never keep the good news about Jesus to ourselves. Who can you share it with today?

Pray

Dear Lord Jesus, You are so amazing. Stronger than death, You have the power to do anything. When times are hard, help us remember that we follow a God who is bigger than our problems. Amen.

Doubted

John 20:24–28

'One of the twelve disciples, Thomas (called the Twin), was not with them when Jesus came. So the other disciples told him, "We have seen the Lord!"

Thomas said to them, "Unless I see the scars of the nails in his hands and put my finger on those scars and my hand in his side, I will not believe."

A week later the disciples were together again indoors, and Thomas was with them. The doors were locked, but Jesus came and stood among them and said, "Peace be with you." Then he said to Thomas, "Put your finger here, and look at my hands; then reach out your hand and put it in my side. Stop your doubting, and believe!"

Thomas answered him, "My Lord and my God!"'

Something to think about

After He came back to life, Jesus went to visit His friends the disciples. Thomas wasn't there and when he heard about Jesus he didn't believe it. His reaction was understandable, because it *does* seems crazy. But Jesus didn't write Thomas off for not believing straightaway; instead He went back and offered to let Thomas put his fingers in the hole in His side, which would have been fairly gross. Thomas didn't do it, as he took one look at Jesus and knew it was Him. He recognised that Jesus was more than he had thought – that He was God.

Sometimes we aren't sure about Jesus. We've not seen Him with our eyes, and there are days when it's hard to believe He is real. Jesus doesn't write us off either, but He does invite us to look closer and see that He definitely is real. It's OK to ask questions, as long as we're really looking for answers.

Bekah says...

Megan is our youngest daughter - she asks questions all the time about everything. It's exhausting sometimes but it is her way of getting to know the world.

Something to talk about

· What questions do you have about Jesus?
· What answers have you found?

Steve's interesting fact

The expression 'doubting Thomas' has made its way into the dictionary because of this story. It refers to someone who refuses to believe something without seeing definite proof of it.

Pray

Dear Lord Jesus, thank You for loving us even on days when we're not sure about You. Please keep revealing Yourself to us. Amen.

Left?

Acts 1:6–9

'When the apostles met together with Jesus, they asked him, "Lord, will you at this time give the Kingdom back to Israel?"

Jesus said to them, "The times and occasions are set by my Father's own authority, and it is not for you to know when they will be. But when the Holy Spirit comes upon you, you will be filled with power, and you will be witnesses for me in Jerusalem, in all of Judea and Samaria, and to the ends of the earth."

After saying this, he was taken up to heaven as they watched him, and a cloud hid him from their sight.'

Something to think about

After Jesus rose again, He didn't stay around on earth for very long – just a few weeks. He had done everything He came to do; He had started the big rescue and now it was time for His followers to tell everyone all about it.

Jesus did the hard part, and now His friends needed to go and tell the rest of the world. It would have been scary for His disciples to see Him go, to think about telling the world about Him, but Jesus promises not to leave them on their own. Instead, He says He's going to send His Holy Spirit to give them power, strength and courage so that they can speak out.

Bekah says...

I hate being left on my own. Recently everyone in my family was away for a fortnight. I hated it and ended up inviting people around every day so that I wasn't alone!

Something to talk about

· Have you ever been left on your own?
· How did you find it?

Steve's interesting fact

On 10 June 2012, David Cameron, the UK's then Prime Minister, accidentally left his daughter behind after a family lunch out! She was only alone for 15 minutes and they were very glad she was still safe when they went back for her!

Something to do together

One of the best things about being part of God's family is never being alone again. Is there someone lonely you could invite to have lunch with you this weekend?

Pray

Dear Jesus, thank You that You didn't leave us on our own, but sent Your Holy Spirit to always be with us. Please help us to find ways to tell those we know about You. Amen.

Empowered

Acts 2:1–6

'When the day of Pentecost came, all the believers were gathered together in one place. Suddenly there was a noise from the sky which sounded like a strong wind blowing, and it filled the whole house where they were sitting. Then they saw what looked like tongues of fire which spread out and touched each person there. They were all filled with the Holy Spirit and began to talk in other languages, as the Spirit enabled them to speak.

There were Jews living in Jerusalem, religious people who had come from every country in the world. When they heard this noise, a large crowd gathered. They were all excited, because all of them heard the believers talking in their own languages.'

Something to think about

We saw last week that Jesus promised that He would send His Spirit to the disciples after He left, so that they would have courage to travel around, telling everyone about what they had experienced and how Jesus had rescued anyone who believes in Him. At Pentecost, Jesus' promise was about to come true, as the Holy Spirit came. It was amazing – the sound of wind and fire on people's heads – just mind-blowing. But it wasn't just an amazing party trick, the Holy Spirit had come to change their lives so they could go and change other people's.

They all started speaking different languages, Peter started explaining everything that had happened, and, by bedtime, 3,000 people had chosen to follow Jesus and been baptised! It was the beginning of something truly amazing.

Steve says...

The Holy Spirit loves to come and fill us. But it's never just about us having a great experience, it's always so that we have power to share His love with other people.

Something to talk about

· Have you ever experienced the Holy Spirit?
· What difference did He make in your life?

Pray

Dear Lord Jesus, thank You for sending the Holy Spirit so that we would never have to be alone. Please send Your Spirit upon us now, to give us the power to change the world for You. Amen.

Brave prayers

Acts 4:27–31

"'For indeed Herod and Pontius Pilate met together in this city with the Gentiles and the people of Israel against Jesus, your holy Servant, whom you made Messiah. They gathered to do everything that you by your power and will had already decided would happen. And now, Lord, take notice of the threats they have made, and allow us, your servants, to speak your message with all boldness. Reach out your hand to heal, and grant that wonders and miracles may be performed through the name of your holy Servant Jesus."

When they finished praying, the place where they were meeting was shaken. They were all filled with the Holy Spirit and began to proclaim God's message with boldness.'

Something to think about

The disciples started telling everyone about Jesus, but some people didn't like what they were doing. It was the same people who hadn't liked what Jesus was doing. Peter and John got arrested and taken to court, where there were people who wanted to kill them (see verses 1–22). It was a dangerous time.

The verses above are a prayer that all the followers of Jesus prayed once Peter and John were released. What is amazing is that they didn't pray for the danger to go away, or for their enemies to disappear, instead they prayed for boldness and courage. They prayed to be stronger people who could overcome their problems.

Bekah says...

When we face problems, it's good to not just ask God to take those problems away. God always wants us to grow - so let's try to ask Him to help us be braver, stronger, kinder, more patient or whatever it is we need.

Something to talk about

· Have you ever faced a really big problem?
· How did you overcome it?

Steve says...

This is one of my favourite quotes, from Nelson Mandela: 'I learned that courage was not the absence of fear, but the triumph over it.'

Bekah says...

Could you write a bold prayer about a problem your family is facing? What do you need God to do in your lives to help you overcome that problem?

Pray

Dear Lord Jesus, thank You for always hearing our prayers. Help us not to always want the easy solution, rather help us to be stronger, bolder people who can overcome our problems with Your help. Amen.

Sharing

Acts 4:32–35

'The group of believers was one in mind and heart. None of them said that any of their belongings were their own, but they all shared with one another everything they had. With great power the apostles gave witness to the resurrection of the Lord Jesus, and God poured rich blessings on them all. There was no one in the group who was in need. Those who owned fields or houses would sell them, bring the money received from the sale, and turn it over to the apostles; and the money was distributed according to the needs of the people.'

Something to think about

The first Christians started the first church and it was a very wonderful place to be. There was danger around from people who didn't like Christians, but they made sure they looked after each other. They were amazing sharers.

People who had a lot of money or land shared what they had with those who had very little. It was a radical way to live. Even in those days, it was normal to want to have a big house and lots of money, but these new Christians thought totally differently. They knew everything they had was a gift from God so they shared with everyone around them, making sure everything was fair.

Bekah says...

Every 50 years, there would be a 'year of jubilee', when people were meant to cancel their debts, give land back and release their slaves so that everyone was equal again (see Leviticus 25). Imagine if our world was like that now!

Something to talk about

· How do you share what God has given you?
· Has sharing ever meant you have had to go without something you would like?

Steve's interesting fact

In a survey* on giving, Myanmar was found to be the most generous country in the world, with over two thirds of the population regularly making donations. The United States came in as the second most giving country, and Australia third.

Bekah says...

Is there something you can do today to help someone in need?

Pray

Father God, You don't like unfairness. It's so easy to be greedy, but we want to share what we have with people who have less than us. Help us to always be kind. Amen.

*Research conducted by the Charities Aid Foundation. See www.futureworldgiving.org/2016

A way through

Acts 5:17–21

'Then the High Priest and all his companions, members of the local party of the Sadducees, became extremely jealous of the apostles; so they decided to take action. They arrested the apostles and put them in the public jail. But that night an angel of the Lord opened the prison gates, led the apostles out, and said to them, "Go and stand in the Temple, and tell the people all about this new life." The apostles obeyed, and at dawn they entered the Temple and started teaching.'

Something to think about

'Apostle' was another name for the original disciples. They were still in danger and got arrested again. This time they got put in prison. It must have felt a bit like their plan was spoiled, but God knew better. His plan to rescue the world was not going to be stopped by some jealous men. So He sent an angel to open the door – how incredible. The apostles weren't put off talking about Jesus so they went right back to telling everyone about Him!

There are times when our plans seem to have hit a dead end and we can't see how they can be fixed. But if we are following Jesus and His plans then we can know that, just like in this story, God has a way through.

Bekah says...

All the best stories have a narrow escape – Simba in The Lion King, Nemo in Finding Nemo, the kids in Despicable Me. They're all great stories, but God's story is full of excitement and narrow escapes too. He is the true hero who rescues His people time and time again.

Something to talk about

· If you could be a superhero, who would you be?
· What's your favourite adventure story?

Steve's interesting fact

We're all used to seeing Superman's good looks and his dark hair, but originally Superman was supposed to be a bald character, obsessed with dominating the world.

Bekah says...

If you were designing a superhero costume for God, what would it look like?

Pray

Father God, You are our hero. Thank You that even when everything seems impossible, You still have a way. Help us to remember that when times are hard so that we trust You. Amen.

WEEK 11:
WHAT HAPPENED
NEXT
FRIDAY

Peer pressure

Acts 5:29–33

'Peter and the other apostles answered, "We must obey God, not men. The God of our ancestors raised Jesus from death, after you had killed him by nailing him to a cross. God raised him to his right side as Leader and Saviour, to give the people of Israel the opportunity to repent and have their sins forgiven. We are witnesses to these things—we and the Holy Spirit, who is God's gift to those who obey him."

When the members of the Council heard this, they were so furious that they wanted to have the apostles put to death.'

Something to think about

When the priests send men to catch the apostles, you'd think the apostles might just do as they're told for a bit. But not these guys. They are getting more and more brave as they see just how great God is. So they stand up to the priests and say they have to listen to God, not men.

We probably don't have priests telling us to do things we shouldn't. But we do get peer pressure – even from our friends sometimes. Wherever we go, we want to fit in, but if that means doing something that doesn't seem to be something Jesus would do, we need to try and be brave like the apostles and say, 'I follow God, not men.'

Bekah says...

One Halloween recently, one of my oldest friends invited me and my girls to her Halloween party. I didn't know what to do – I didn't want to offend my friend but I knew that going wasn't right either. In the end I was brave and told her I was really sorry, but we couldn't go because we don't like celebrating Halloween.

Something to talk about

· When have you faced peer pressure?
· When have you stood up against it?

Steve's interesting fact

I've heard that children and teens who give in to peer pressure are more likely to experience a loss of their individuality. As a result, their favourite movies, clothes, music, may be determined by someone else instead of their own individual taste.

Pray

Father God, we love You, and want to grow to be more and more like You. Help us to be strong even when our friends are encouraging us to do things You wouldn't like. Help us to be brave enough to say no when it matters. Amen.

Staying calm

Acts 6:12–15

'They seized Stephen and took him before the Council. Then they brought in some men to tell lies about him. "This man," they said, "is always talking against our sacred Temple and the Law of Moses. We heard him say that this Jesus of Nazareth will tear down the Temple and change all the customs which have come down to us from Moses!" All those sitting in the Council fixed their eyes on Stephen and saw that his face looked like the face of an angel.'

Something to think about

Stephen was a great man who helped the apostles. He got caught and arrested by people who hated Jesus and those who followed Him.

What happened to Stephen was totally unfair, but he didn't become angry or violent; he knew the truth and that God knew the truth. So he stayed calm and peaceful.

Bekah says...

I hate when things aren't fair. It makes me want to fight and fix it. But this story is a lesson in being like Jesus even when people are being mean. Jesus was the same when He got taken to court. He stayed calm and polite no matter what happened (see Matthew 27:11–14). We need to try and be the same.

Something to talk about
· Has anyone ever got you in trouble?
· How did you react?

Steve's interesting fact
The apostles had found that they needed helpers to look after the care of the widows and the poor, so they ordained seven deacons (see Acts 6:1–7). Stephen is the most famous of these, and his name means 'crown'. He was the first follower of Jesus to die for his faith (see Acts 6:54–60).

Something to do together
Why not try this game together? Sit in a circle and choose who is going to go first. That person has to focus on someone and try to make them smile by saying, 'Baby, if you love me, give me a big smile.' You can use a silly voice, pull a funny face or anything to make them smile. They have to do their best to keep their face straight, no matter what you do! If they smile, it's their turn. If not, you go again.

Pray
Dear Lord Jesus, You never let other people's actions make You be unkind or rude. Help us to be like You and Stephen, showing Your love no matter how unkind people are to us. Amen.

Magic

Acts 8:9–13

'A man named Simon lived there, who for some time had astounded the Samaritans with his magic. He claimed that he was someone great, and everyone in the city, from all classes of society, paid close attention to him. "He is that power of God known as 'The Great Power,'" they said. They paid this attention to him because for such a long time he had astonished them with his magic. But when they believed Philip's message about the good news of the Kingdom of God and about Jesus Christ, they were baptized, both men and women. Simon himself also believed; and after being baptized, he stayed close to Philip and was astounded when he saw the great wonders and miracles that were being performed.'

Something to think about

Simon was a magician – he could do amazing things that looked like magic. No one could work out how he did it. They thought he had special powers and they loved to watch what he did.

There was nothing really magic about Simon. When Philip came along and Simon heard about Jesus, he realised he was hearing about someone with real power and so chose to follow Jesus. When he saw the miracles the disciples did in Jesus' name, Simon knew they were more than tricks, more than he could ever do. He recognised that he had seen something really amazing and that it could only come from God.

Steve says...

I do magic tricks. I can pull rabbits out of hats, make things disappear and read people's minds. But really it's all tricks and I've no special powers. But I have seen God do amazing miracles – things that no man could ever do. Like Simon, I know God's power is real.

Something to talk about

· What's the best magic trick you've ever seen?
· How do you think the magician did it?

Steve's interesting fact

The largest illusion ever staged was performed by multi-millionaire American magician, David Copperfield, who created the illusion of vanishing the Statue of Liberty in New York, on his TV special in 1983.

Pray

Father God, You are amazing. With You, nothing is impossible. Help us to understand the difference between a trick and Your mighty power. Amen.

Enemy

Acts 9:1–6

'In the meantime, Saul kept up his violent threats of murder against the followers of the Lord. He went to the High Priest and asked for letters of introduction to the synagogues in Damascus, so that if he should find there any followers of the Way of the Lord, he would be able to arrest them, both men and women, and bring them back to Jerusalem.

As Saul was coming near the city of Damascus, suddenly a light from the sky flashed around him. He fell to the ground and heard a voice saying to him, "Saul, Saul! Why do you persecute me?"

"Who are you, Lord?" he asked.

"I am Jesus, whom you persecute," the voice said. "But get up and go into the city, where you will be told what you must do."'

Something to think about

The news about Jesus was beginning to spread – just the way He told His disciples that it should. But some of the Jewish priests were getting more and more angry about it. Saul was a Pharisee, a Jewish teacher, and he was determined to stop the news spreading any further. He wanted to put the Christians in prison, and do whatever it took to make them be quiet.

But God had another plan. He knew that Saul simply hadn't recognised that Jesus was the rescuer God had been promising, so he introduced him personally in a way that meant Saul really had no choice but to recognise Jesus.

Bekah says...

Saul was a violent man, who hurt people who disagreed with him. But Jesus saw potential in Saul, and went to meet this frightening man.

Something to talk about
· Who frightens you?
· Can you imagine them becoming friends with God?

Steve says...

Why not look at some current news stories and pray for the people in them to know Jesus and have their lives changed?

Pray
Father God, thank You that no one is too evil to change and become Your friend. Thank You that no matter what we do, You still want to meet us and give us a chance to change. Help us to see potential in the people we meet. Amen.

Speaking up

Acts 22:12–16

'In that city was a man named Ananias, a religious man who obeyed our Law and was highly respected by all the Jews living there. He came to me, stood by me, and said, "Brother Saul, see again!" At that very moment I saw again and looked at him. He said, "The God of our ancestors has chosen you to know his will, to see his righteous Servant, and to hear him speaking with his own voice. For you will be a witness for him to tell everyone what you have seen and heard. And now, why wait any longer? Get up and be baptized and have your sins washed away by praying to him."'

Something to think about

This is the next part of Saul's story. A Christian man, Ananias, went to tell Saul all about Jesus and help him see again. Earlier in Acts we are told that when God asked Ananias to visit Saul, he didn't want to go because he was so scared (see Acts 9:10–16). He knew how dangerous Saul was. But, even though he was frightened, Ananias listened to God, obeyed Him and then was friendly to an enemy – he even called him 'brother'.

Ananias trusted that God knew best so he went to what was a life-changing meeting for Saul. Ananias' bravery meant that Saul, an enemy of Jesus, became one of his best friends and went on to tell everyone he met about Him.

Bekah says...

I once prayed for God to give me an opportunity to tell someone about Jesus. The next day, a supplier at work rang up and asked if I would go for lunch and tell him all about my faith!

Something to talk about

· When have you had an opportunity to tell someone about Jesus?
· What fears stop you from talking about Him more?

Steve says...

I was on a mission trip in Paris and visited the Eiffel Tower one evening. Coming down in the elevator I figured I had a captive audience for 45 seconds so, in a loud voice, I thanked everyone for joining me and then shared my faith. It was too good an opportunity to miss.

Pray

Dear Lord Jesus, You are our best friend. Help us to be brave enough to introduce You to our other friends so that they can learn to love You too. Amen.

Changed

Acts 9:19–22

'Saul stayed for a few days with the believers in Damascus. He went straight to the synagogues and began to preach that Jesus was the Son of God.

All who heard him were amazed and asked, "Isn't he the one who in Jerusalem was killing those who worship that man Jesus? And didn't he come here for the very purpose of arresting those people and taking them back to the chief priests?"

But Saul's preaching became even more powerful, and his proofs that Jesus was the Messiah were so convincing that the Jews who lived in Damascus could not answer him.'

Something to think about

Saul was a passionate man who never did anything by halves. He went from number one enemy to number one supporter overnight. He didn't hang around just enjoying his new friendship with Jesus; he started telling everyone he met about it straightaway. People could hardly believe their ears!

Sometimes we act like Jesus is just our friend while we are at home. But He wants us to be like Saul, talking about Him everywhere we go. When we choose to follow Jesus, our whole lives should change, just like Saul's did, so that people around us are amazed at the difference and can see what Jesus is doing in our lives.

Bekah says...

My mum ran a youth club for 40 years. One Christmas she gave them a party and one of the boys from the local estate asked her why she did so much for him when no one else cared. She told him it was because she shared Jesus' love for him. He could see the difference Jesus made in her life.

Something to talk about

· How has being a follower of Jesus changed you?
· What do you think God wants to change in you today?

Steve's interesting fact

Saul did everything he could to try and stop the growth of Christianity. In fact, when Stephen was killed, Saul was there, watching the cloaks of those who were stoning Stephen (see Acts 7:57–58). How much he had changed!

Pray

Father God, thank You for loving us as we are, with all our faults and flaws. But thank You that You also want to help us grow to be more like You. Help us to live lives that show people that You are constantly at work in us. Amen.

For everyone

Acts 10:9–16

'The next day, as they were on their way and coming near Joppa, Peter went up on the roof of the house about noon in order to pray. He became hungry and wanted something to eat; while the food was being prepared, he had a vision. He saw heaven opened and something coming down that looked like a large sheet being lowered by its four corners to the earth. In it were all kinds of animals, reptiles, and wild birds. A voice said to him, "Get up, Peter; kill and eat!"

But Peter said, "Certainly not, Lord! I have never eaten anything ritually unclean or defiled."

The voice spoke to him again, "Do not consider anything unclean that God has declared clean." This happened three times, and then the thing was taken back up into heaven.'

Something to think about

This is a slightly weird story about a dream. To understand it, you need to know two things first. Before Jesus came, you could only really know God if you were a Jew. And Jews could only eat certain animals.

This dream was to let Peter and the other Christians know that because of Jesus everything had changed. Firstly, the rules about food had gone, but, more importantly still, God wanted them to know that the good news about Jesus was for everyone, not just Jews.

The great news of this dream was that it didn't matter who your mum and dad were, which country you came from – not even what religion you were following. Anyone could meet Jesus and choose to follow Him.

Bekah says...

When I was 15, I canoed down this incredible gorge with my French pen-friend and her cousins. It was the most amazing journey, but no one really talked to me because I was the outsider.

Something to talk about

· Have you ever been left out?
· How good are you at including other people?

Steve's interesting fact

Dreams are responsible for many of the greatest inventions of humankind: Larry Page's idea for Google, James Watson's double helix spiral structure of a DNA chain, and Elias Howe's idea for the sewing machine.

Bekah says...

Is there someone who you can include today who often gets left out?

Pray

Dear Lord Jesus, thank You for changing everything. Thank You for being good news for the whole world. Amen.

Famous!

Acts 14:8–11,14–15

'In Lystra there was a crippled man who had been lame from birth and had never been able to walk. He sat there and listened to Paul's words. Paul saw that he believed and could be healed, so he looked straight at him and said in a loud voice, "Stand up straight on your feet!" The man jumped up and started walking around. When the crowds saw what Paul had done, they started shouting in their own Lycaonian language, "The gods have become like men and have come down to us!"

When Barnabas and Paul heard what they were about to do, they tore their clothes and ran into the middle of the crowd, shouting, "Why are you doing this? We ourselves are only human beings like you!"'

Something to think about

Paul in this story is the Saul that we read about earlier in the week – God changed his name along with his character! By this time, Paul was travelling far and wide telling people about Jesus and doing incredible miracles. But some people misunderstood and didn't realise it was God's Holy Spirit doing the miracles, they thought Paul and his friend Barnabas were gods themselves.

It could have been tempting for Paul and Barnabas to enjoy all the special treatment, but they didn't want to distract attention from God. They weren't performing miracles to make themselves look good. They were performing miracles so that people could see that God is real.

Bekah says...

One of our daughters once asked if we'd be proud of her if she became famous. We said it rather depended on why! Just being well known isn't something to aim for; living lives that point to Jesus is far better.

Something to talk about
· Who do you really admire?
· What would you love to be famous for?

Steve's interesting fact
Singers, actors and TV presenters feature heavily in the top 20 of UK Twitter accounts. Between them they have a staggering 345 million followers, with One Direction still coming out on top, even while on a 'break', with 31.4 million followers.

Something to do together
Could you each find something kind to do in secret this weekend, without telling the rest of your family what it is?

Pray
Dear Lord, in everything we do, help us to worry less about what people think of us and more about what they think of You. Amen.

Bible reading notes designed especially
for each member of the family

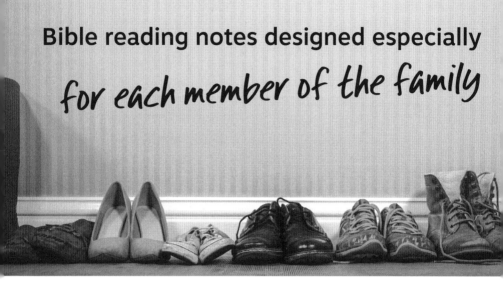

With six different titles available as one-year subscriptions, you and everyone in your family can be inspired on their own faith journey every day of the year. Choose your way of engaging with the Bible:

Insightful and encouraging Bible reading notes for men and women

Practical and relevant daily guidance for teenagers

Fun and engaging daily readings for children

| Every Day with Jesus | Inspiring Women Every Day | Life Every Day (Jeff Lucas) | Mettle 15–18s | YP's 11–14s | Topz 7–11s |

For more information, current prices and to order a one-year subscription, visit **www.cwr.org.uk/subscriptions** or call **01252 784700**
Also available from Christian bookshops.

Waverley Abbey College

Courses and seminars

Publishing and media

Conference facilities

Transforming lives

CWR's vision is to enable people to experience personal transformation through applying God's Word to their lives and relationships.

Our Bible-based training and resources help people around the world to:
- Grow in their walk with God
- Understand and apply Scripture to their lives
- Resource themselves and their church
- Develop pastoral care and counselling skills
- Train for leadership
- Strengthen relationships, marriage and family life and much more.

Our insightful writers provide daily Bible reading notes and other resources for all ages, and our experienced course designers and presenters have gained an international reputation for excellence and effectiveness.

CWR's Training and Conference Centres in Surrey and East Sussex, England, provide excellent facilities in idyllic settings – ideal for both learning and spiritual refreshment.

CWR Applying God's Word
to everyday life and relationships

CWR, Waverley Abbey House,
Waverley Lane, Farnham,
Surrey GU9 8EP, UK

Telephone: **+44 (0)1252 784700**
Email: **info@cwr.org.uk**
Website: **www.cwr.org.uk**

Registered Charity No. 294387
Company Registration No. 1990308

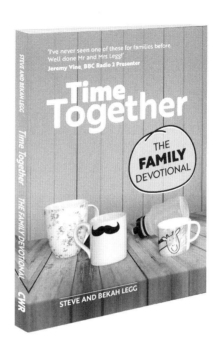

Continue bringing your family together

Enjoy even more shared, daily experiences of the Bible with *Time Together: The Family Devotional.*

In the follow-up to *All Together*, spend another 12 weeks discovering the stories of Noah, Abraham, Ruth, King David and others, as well as a closer look at the Psalms, the Christmas story, and people who encountered Jesus in the Bible.

Each day of this devotional includes a short Bible reading, along with thoughts and questions that open up Scripture and spark conversation.

Authors: Steve and Bekah Legg

ISBN: 978-1-78259-798-8